Why We Serve

Douglas Fisher, editor

Why We Serve

Personal Stories of Catholic Lay Ministers

paulist press   *new york/ramsey*

Library of Congress
Catalog Card Number: 84-80360

ISBN: 0-8091-2640-0

Published by Paulist Press
545 Island Road, Ramsey, N.J. 07446

Printed and bound in the
United States of America

Contents

Rosemary Haughton

Preface

The conventional phrase is used in official Church documents, sermons and pastoral letters: "This is the age of the laity." Vocations to ordained ministry and religious orders are declining, for good or ill. The vast system which depended on them falters. So the talk is of lay people. "You are the Church." You are expected to fill the gaps, keep the system running by doing work that sisters and priests can't do. So lay people have found themselves teaching religion, organizing liturgy, going abroad to serve or support in foreign missions. When all this began, and for a time, the sense of newness and responsibility was exciting and satisfying.

At a certain point, something changed. People discovered they had ideas of their own, saw different ways to do things. Lay people studied Scripture, prayed together, shared dreams. They felt the call that would not let them rest; they wanted to be ministers of good news, carrying the mission of Christ to a despairing world. "Vocation" was a word they began to use about themselves as well. Suddenly, the whole picture was different. Lay people are hearing that this is "the age of the laity" and "you are the Church" and taking those phrases seriously. They have listened to the voice they hear in the Gospels and in the world, and responded.

It can be an uncomfortable experience. People find themselves feeling and thinking differently; when they share their

vii

thoughts their friends and families are dismayed or disapprov-
ing. Parents tacitly or openly hope they will "get over it" and
"settle down." Even pastors and spiritual directors become un-
easy and talk of "waiting on God" which really means doing
nothing. One woman, who later became the foundress of a
whole movement of lay missionaries, was told to go home and
pray for two years, to become a sister, in general to shut up
and go away. Fortunately, she did not.

What we are experiencing is not simply a continuance of
the same system with different operators. The movement of
lay people into mission means a rediscovery of the meaning of
the Church. It happens in two ways. One way is that people
move forward to fill gaps in the system, and in doing so discover inadequacies in the system. They work, pray, reflect
with others, come up with new ways, and—more importantly—begin to understand this role differently, ask new
questions, break old patterns. They perceive the mission of the
Church less as a matter of maintaining itself and more as a mission of transformation, not just of the Church but of the
world. They go back to the Gospels and discover there a man
with a mission of transformation, who challenged accepted
ideas, broke categories, proposed new ways—not in rejection
of his tradition but in the name of what was most essential to
it. As they struggle, share, study, suffer and move forward
they encounter those who come to this rediscovery the other
way, those who have been disillusioned, alienated in their tradition, unwilling to get involved in a Church that seems to
them to have lost touch in many ways with the mission of Jesus. Many, feeling like this, simply withdraw into a limbo of
mingled resentment or nostalgia, but others struggle with their
situation, pray, read, talk to others, and seek a way to understand Church that will enable them to claim their tradition as
their own. They, too, are impelled by the Spirit who will not
leave them alone.

Together, such people represent a new birth. They are intelligent, aware, leaders and initiators. Some have little formal education, some a great deal. As in the beginning of the Gospel they meet in the discovery of that Gospel calling. They cannot rest while a world of people waits for some kind of hope, some sense that they matter, that they have a future. These people are the shoots of the new Church, growing from the deep roots which have nourished so many new ventures in the Christian centuries—most of them questioned and even persecuted at the time, though history has justified and affirmed them. New growth is never easy. It displaces some older things, absorbs others, changes most of them. It is controversial. But so was Jesus and so were all his closest followers. Whatever the struggles, we know that this strange and terrifying time in human history, pregnant with possibility yet under threat of death, demands a different kind of Christian response, a response of courage, freedom and vision. This book presents a little of the concrete experience of those who are trying to respond.

Foreword

Last October I made my ad limina visit to Rome. It was a great honor for this blacksmith's son to visit with our Holy Father, John Paul II. The visit was especially meaningful to me because in our diocese we had just completed a synod and I could share the excitement with my father, the Pope. I told him how we had worked out a vision for our diocese and set a direction we could work toward for the next ten years. When I described the process of our synod and the share lay men and women had in developing synod policies, John Paul responded enthusiastically. "When I was a bishop in Poland we had a synod," he said, "but it was only for the priests and bishop. Your synod was much better because it involved the laity. The Church is the people of God!"

Certainly "people of God" is the phrase more than any other that expresses what the Second Vatican Council has meant to the Church. In *Lumen Gentium* the Council fathers spoke of the "new people of God, born of water and the Holy Spirit, this people established as a chosen race, a royal priesthood, a holy nation whose heritage is the dignity and freedom of the children of God. . . ." How radical! How thrilling! A new day for all of us! And yet how fearful and shocking!

"People of God," however, is not all of the story of *Lumen Gentium*. I remember several years ago when I was chairman of the Bishops' Committee on the Laity. I was giving a report to the Administrative Committee of NCCB on the progress we had been making in calling laity to ministry and decision making in the Church. I was leaning heavily on the "people of God" theme when one of the bishops interrupted: "Remember, Bishop, it is a hierarchical people of God." Right he was.

In Chapter III *Lumen Gentium* firmly establishes the hierarchical image of Church. "For the nurturing and constant growth of the people of God, Christ the Lord instituted in his Church a variety of ministries which work for the good of the whole body. For those ministers who are endowed with sacred powers are servants of their brothers so that all who are of the people of God can work toward a common goal freely and in an orderly way."

The seeming ambiguity between Chapters II and III has been the source of a great deal of confusion. Just how much are we people of God, how much hierarchical? Nowhere in the Church is this more keenly felt than in the call of laity to ministry.

In every parish where there is an ounce of pastoral encouragement lay women and men are responding with eagerness to opportunities for ministry. It's as though there is something in the air, some instinct for a new day in the Church. A host of examples could be cited. Several years ago, for example, I visited the Divinity School at Yale University and talked with some thirty Catholic students enrolled there. They were so committed to working full-time for the Church that they were pursuing degrees in theology. Most of them had no idea whether jobs would be waiting for them.

This is our dilemma as Church. The numbers of priests and religious are diminishing at an alarming rate. Great numbers of laity feel called to take up the slack. As Church we do not know how to make the switch. Our structures are highly clerical. We have much difficulty accepting laity into ministry. We do not know how to find the money to pay professionals a decent salary for their services. We are reluctant to give volunteers the programs of skills training and formation to qualify them for leadership.

As you read *Why We Serve*, you will share the experience of laity who are administering as professionals or volunteers in today's Church. They know the agony and ecstasy of serving in a Church in transition, a Church crippled by clericalism, a Church confused about its identity. They complain of low pay, apathy among priests and bishops, lack of status and support. *Why We Serve*, however, is in no way a lament. The stories are full of joy, faith, eagerness. The message is that, thank God, lay ministers are here to stay.

Megan McKenna, one of the authors, says it best: "This is the reality of lay ministry: usually unrecognized, unacknowledged, half believed in, non-validated, sometimes caught between a rock and a hard place, a place of exhilaration and surrender, surprise, miracles and endurance. It is a place of confusion and possibility, a place where one endures as much from one's church as from the world. This ministry is not ordained, but it is charismatic, tightly bound in tradition and new forms. It is ministry that anyone can do; it is power enfleshed in just about anybody."

I love this book. If you are tired of reading treatises on lay ministry, you will be delighted to meet some exciting people who preach what they practice. Some volunteers, some full-time professionals, they teach, they counsel, they organize, they lead parishes, they work in the missions, they clown. I think of Paul, "There are different gifts, but the same Spirit; there are different ministries but the same Lord" (1 Cor 12:4). There is a richness in the ministries that engage these fourteen storytellers that must enliven the clerical Church. People could see Christ in a Church where laity, religious and priests minister side by side in an atmosphere of dignity and respect.

I like to quote Bishop Neves, a former Vice-President of the Pontifical Council of the Laity: "This is my deepest conviction, namely, that the layman is a man (woman) of the Church living within the world to build there the communities of the people of God, and a man (woman) of the world living within the Church to make heard the questions, the aspirations, the problems and the conflicts which run through the world."

What we are truly about as Church is building the Kingdom of God in our world. I hunger so for that Kingdom to come. To do that our Church must image ever more completely what Jesus wants it to be. The stories of these fourteen ministers tell me that as people of God we have come farther than we think.

Introduction

The idea for this book grew out of a conversation which took place at a religious education congress. This dialogue happened at lunch with a young man sitting on one side of me and an older man on the other. The young man said, "I'm studying for a master's in theology with the goal of obtaining a job in parish ministry. I really feel the Lord is calling me to both marriage and ministry within the structure of the Church. It is great to be a part of the Church at a time when a person can do both and make a living through ministry."

After the young man left, the older man said, "Another example of naive idealism. There is an awful lot of romanticism around lay ministry these days. Everyone starts out with this great missionary zeal—to say nothing of the time and money they put into a degree. Then when they confront living a life of near poverty, with jobs which demand so much time that there is little left for the family, with all manner of restrictions on what they can do and decide because they are not ordained, they turn to something else in frustration."

Who had the truth? Was the young man dooming himself to a life of unappreciated hard work, unrealistic expectations, family conflict and an unsatisfactory standard of living? Or should his enthusiasm be applauded and supported? What is lay ministry really like?

The best answer to those questions come from lay ministers themselves. They live out the day-to-day reality. This book is a forum for some lay ministers to say what ministry really is, in the way it is lived now. The basis of this book is experience. It is truly a "story theology" as ministers reveal an ecclesiology and spirituality which is implicit in their personal journeys. The challenge is left to the reader to draw conclusions from these life stories.

The reader should be aware of two arbitrary elements in this book. One is the definition of lay ministry. In canvassing the country looking for authors, my criteria was for people who worked full-time for the Catholic Church in a non-ordained capacity and relied on ministry as their sole means of financial support. This is one narrow view of lay ministry which I used for the sake of unity in these stories. Some would say that anything done in the name of Jesus Christ is ministry or that all are called to ministry. Others, who fit the category which I laid out, do not want the label "lay minister." They feel that it causes a gradation within the Church between them and the non-ordained. It is not my purpose to argue definitions. All have valid points. My only purpose was to gather the stories of full-time, non-ordained Catholic ministers who earn their livelihood through ministry. To this category of people I gave the inadequate label "lay ministers."

The second arbitrary variable within this book is its scope of ministries. You will find here a vast range, from DRE to pastor to teacher to clown to social justice prophet. There are far more ministries still. Book size limits us to what is here.

These personal stories are held together by a common theme: cooperation with the Spirit. In telling their life stories with all the joys and frustrations, what this editor saw was a people who listen to the Spirit within their lives and respond creatively. It is a listening which demands constant evaluation and conversion. For these people, that listening, converting, and responding has led to full lives for themselves and service to others. From this book the lay minister or future lay minister or interested observer might be able to glean what lay ministry is and where it is going. And every reader will do that differently. What I hope all readers will find here are people attempting to live the Gospel in the way they hear the Spirit calling them. In so doing they challenge us to look at the choices of our hearts.

What If Someone Asks Me What I Do?

What is it like to have a career in the Church as a layperson? Here's an example.

I'm going to a party at a friend's home—a mixed group of various professions, cultural and religious backgrounds, interests, and life-styles. My greatest fear is not that I may have bad breath or whether my hair will look O.K. Terror comes with the thought, "What if someone asks me what I do?" As I put on my nylons, choose my jewelry and decide on a hairstyle, the thought comes, "I could lie, or simply say I'm in education." Well, experience has taught that I'm a lousy liar and the second option never satisfies. So I opt for truth and vow to talk a lot about movies, food, and how lousy the weather has been.

The party is great—good food and conversation. I strike up a conversation with an interesting man who talks a bit about his law practice. My nerves start to jitter as I await the inevitable question about to spill out of his mouth. I consider my options—I could excuse myself for the powder room or to get more ice in my drink. I could tell a funny joke, nonchalantly move into another group of people, have a coughing attack, or spill my drink. "Oh, maybe it won't be so bad—I do have an interesting job, so why *not* talk about it?" My prediction comes true, "And what line of work are you in, Katie?"

"I'm a director of religious education for St. Mary's parish."
"Oh, I see," comes the response.

There are a variety of possibilities at this point. If he's Catholic, all I have to do is say CCD and the lightbulb goes on. This is the advantage of conversing with people of similar faith. However, it's not without its disadvantages, especially if the person no longer goes to church. Then I might be dumped with the build-up of a guilt-ridden conscience and all the rationalizations why he sleeps in on Sunday mornings and what he sees wrong with the Church today.

Protestants have better models of lay involvement (ministers marry and lead "normal" lives), so the hurdle with them is to explain what my job entails. "I'm in charge of the religious education program for our parish," would be my next line. The response might be, "What *else* do you do?" That is as likely to come from Catholics as from non-Catholics.

Then other people are truly fascinated as to why anyone would choose to do this type of work. When I think about it, and these conversations often give me much food for thought, I do ask myself, "Why do you do this?"

Closer examination of this question reveals a sense of call and commitment, my feeling that ministry is the right place for me. I like the work, it has its challenges, and my deep satisfaction in doing something that is meaningful seems to keep the moments of frustration from overwhelming me completely.

My involvement as a lay minister has had its own metamorphosis. I began upon graduation from college as a parish director of religious education. I had been involved in various aspects of my parish through high school and college but I also enjoyed participating in campus ministry at school. I never really wanted to do anything else but work in the Church. I considered social work, but I saw red tape and bureaucracy getting in my way of helping people. I knew whatever career I chose I wanted to work with people. Through my four years of studying theology and investigating an array of possibilities, I settled on parish work as my starting place.

I loved being a DRE. It was hard work and very demanding. In time I began to see my own tendency toward workaholism which ministry often breeds. I rebelled against being married to my job and decided to live a reasonably human existence that allowed for other outlets besides work.

Observing these traits in myself, I am convinced that people (whether priest, religious, or lay) in ministry are very susceptible to compulsive work and martyr complexes. These patterns are nurtured by the fact that there is so much work that needs to be done and that could be done. A basic problem I observed in ministry is our tendency to take ourselves too seriously. When I would get to the point of being very "hyper" about something that was going wrong or feeling extremely pressured, I used to ask myself: "Will the world fall apart if this doesn't get done?" That question seemed to put it in perspective for me, and I could see that I was making my entire self-worth contigent upon the role I played or task I performed. When I took a closer look I discovered that I was worthwhile and graced long before I entered this profession and that it was self-destructive to consider my job as the sum total of who I was. I have a friend who often tells me, "Lighten up, Katie!" It's good advice, and I have learned to be more playful with life and try to enjoy people for who they are. I no longer have an "agenda." I'll admit, though, that laughter comes hard when it's a week before CCD classes start and three teachers are still needed, or when I have fifteen phone calls to make and while, yes, I'd really like to talk longer, I'd also like to get home before midnight because I've forgotten what my apartment looks like and my cat whines with loneliness. I believe there will always be a tension between our own needs and the needs of our job, and this in part is why I left

parish work to return to full-time study. Leaving the confines
of work responsibility was tremendously liberating but at the
same time frightening because no one needed me anymore. I
had derived a great deal of satisfaction from being the only one
who could answer all the teachers' questions in those fifteen
minutes before classes started. I found myself without a ministerial role and studying in a program that aimed not only to
teach me factual data, but also to challenge me to integrate my
learning into my own life and experience.

After several months of study and reflecting back over
where I'd been, I began to feel the need to move into a new
area rather than to return to parish religious education. My
current involvement in ministry is even more difficult to explain than the job of DRE. My energies are concentrated on
developing means of enabling adults to grow while realizing
the beauty of their lives. I do free-lance work with individuals
and groups in various settings. I am a part-time faculty member at the Institute of Pastoral Studies at Loyola University of
Chicago where my skills are utilized in support services for
students. I am a resource person for an on-going singles program at a local retreat center and I am also in training to become a journal consultant for the Intensive Journal program
developed by Dr. Ira Progoff. Being self-employed allows me
tremendous freedom, but free-lance work has been more demanding than anything I've ever done. The lack of financial
security and a professional support group, and my need to be
totally self-motivated and disciplined in my writing and research, all make my life difficult. Still being quite new to this,
I experience a hand-to-mouth existence and live a simple lifestyle. Sacrifice is part of the fabric of my dreams, and as the
tapestry grows more vivid, what I have given up becomes a
gift rather than a loss.

I don't feel that I've left the field of religious education as much as I've shifted my emphasis. The skills and strengths that religious education developed in me are still very much with me, and I could never work on my own without the model of structure and organization that being a DRE gave to me.

The underlying transition in my life has been one of finding new means of self-expression and choosing to have my work involved in that process. Being free of structure and impediments that arise in any institution has unleashed the creative process within me in ways I never thought possible. But there is an exchange here because it was the uncovering of untapped creativity that led me down this road initially.

The commitment I made in college to go into ministry seems to still be with me even though I feel more like I'm charting unknown territory. The call, though it had an internal dimension before, now seems to come completely from that deeper part of me. What I desire to do is allow those internal stirrings to find expression through my writing, programs I develop and creative works (painting, clay, poetry, and stories). I'm finding a market for this ministry but not without much hard work and a great deal of persistence. The striking difference between my work today and that of being a DRE is that there seem to be no limits now. As I said earlier, working within institutional boundaries has its parameters. Structure is helpful in that it gave me some sense of what I am expected to do, but I found those borders in the way of my creativity. My work's major drawback is the danger of drifting aimlessly without ever really landing on shore. What helps keep me close to land is an inner sense that I have a contribution to make and only by tangible results will new inroads be made. This gift has been graciously made known to me by exploration of the wonder of my life and a deep connection with the mystery that not only lies within me but rests in the beyond and calls me ever forth in my unfolding. I step forward timidly, but resting surely, grounded in the sense that it is here I belong and grateful for all that has led me to this point.

My journey has been enriched and given meaning by the tradition of faith I have been part of, but there has been a deeply personal exploration in which I had to stand alone and find the wisdom that lies within my soul. In discovering that wisdom, the principles that Christianity stood for took on a new dimension and I was able to embrace my tradition with deeper insight and a greater sense of commitment.

In closing, I choose the words of Rainer Maria Rilke whose writings have had a tremendous influence on me. This passage says a great deal for me and perhaps it may give some guidance to those who wonder about their own commitment in the Church:

> I know no advice for you save this: go into yourself and test the deeps in which your life takes rise; at its source you will find the answer to the question whether you *must* create. Accept it, just as it sounds, without inquiring into it. Perhaps it will turn out that you are called to be an artist. Then take that destiny upon yourself and bear it, its burden and its greatness, without ever asking what recompense might come from the outside . . . .
>
> . . . and after all I do only want to advise you to keep growing quietly and seriously throughout your whole development; you cannot disturb it more rudely than by looking outward and expecting from outside replies to questions that only your inmost feeling in your most hushed hour can perhaps answer. (From *Letters to a Young Poet*, pp. 20–21, W.W. Norton and Co. 1954)

Home Missions

> The apostolate of the laity is organized in Catholic Action
> and in other forms of apostolic activity approved by the
> Church; but apart from these, there can be and actually
> are lay apostles, men and women who see all the good to
> be done and the possibilities and means of doing it; and
> they do it with only one desire: the winning of souls to
> truth and grace. (Address of Pope Pius XII to the World
> Congress of the Lay Apostolate on Its Need Today, Oc-
> tober 14, 1951)

While sitting in an education class in 1960 at the University of
Portland, a Holy Cross institution in Portland, Oregon, I
heard a guest priest talk about Volunteer Teacher Mission
Service headquartered in Killeen, Texas. I took the VTMS
brochure home and left it in a drawer until I was ready to decide my future. My practice teaching in a public elementary
school wasn't going well; only the encouragement of the prac-
ticum teacher made me reconsider the profession; and a
teacher contract offer from the Portland public schools reinforced my "worthiness" as a candidate for teaching which I
wasn't feeling called to during the later weeks of my practi-
cum.

    During a retreat at the end of the semester I decided to
join VTMS. In later years I had to admit that I joined for
mostly wrong reasons: a new beginning after discovering that

I wasn't an instant success in the business world following my term of service with the Air Force (1955–58); a return to Texas where my nostalgia recalled the comfort and prestige of my Air Force duty as a navigator who had acquired a Cadillac and shared an apartment in a San Antonio suburb with another lieutenant; guilt for having hurt or cheated some people, and thus a need to "atone for my sins." I had no desire to win souls to truth and grace. I came to fulfill my own needs.

Like some others who joined VTMS, I wasn't well prepared for my assignment as a science, math and physical education teacher for various levels of the sixth through ninth grades at St. Joseph's Junior High in Killeen. Many of us thought we'd be teaching in some poverty school. Instead we taught mostly children of Army personnel who, in many cases, had seen more of this planet than any of us. Sooner or later we discovered some of our inadequacies for our teaching assignment: outdated books or insufficient equipment, inadequate academic preparation for the subjects we taught, and inability to evaluate our own performance or even judge the attainability of the goals for us. One colleague didn't last until Thanksgiving of my first year, due to lack of background for teaching sixth to eighth grade math. My background for teaching science to seventh, eighth and ninth graders was limited to college chemistry and zoology, plus the astronomy and electronics acquired in the Air Force navigation school. We were cripples trying to coach students in a race to academic achievement and Christian commitment.

All of us taught our homeroom religion class, because the large majority were Catholic college graduates who had completed the required religion courses for graduation. What we didn't know about the recent theology of the Church or methodology of teaching religion, we were given at evening courses in the parish. Nothing similar was offered us in other subjects for which we lacked background.

What some of us soon discovered in the sharing of our "prayers, works, joys and sorrows" was that we were becoming a family of friends—a Christian community. We learned that each of us had some gift, some strength or weakness to share with each other. We may not have been able to articulate that at the time, but it was manifest in the support and encouragement coming from others of the group when we lost faith in our ability to teach or see progress in our students. At other times we enjoyed being together simply for meals, outings or worship. We became brothers and sisters in Christ, because he had called us to this "family" supporting our need for acceptance and affirmation.

VTMS, co-founded in 1958 by two Holy Cross priests, Joseph Haley and Fred Underwood, provided more than a worksite to launch our "lay apostolate," the official Church designation for lay ministry of that pre-Vatican II era. From the beginning in 1958 until he resigned as spiritual director in 1962, Fr. Underwood visited each Texas worksite monthly to bring us together for worship, for seminars to discuss some aspect of spiritual growth, and for resolution of conflicts that may have developed between persons within the group or with a supervisor outside the group. Although the entire membership (seventy-five at its peak in 1962–63) came together once a year for a few days of orientation, we met regionally more often, usually at the call of the director; but sometimes members initiated a get-together for mostly social reasons. Those gatherings helped bond together the larger Christian community of VTMS during which we discovered the appreciation we had for one another, the uniqueness of how we were called and how we served.

Among our other discoveries, we found that we could lay aside our middle-class comforts, at least temporarily, to live simply. Our food stipend of $25 a month per person was usually enough when pooled. I rarely heard anyone complain

about the food, the living quarters, or other conditions, except
for the summer heat in the Texas worksites. Many of us had to
adjust to less bedroom space than we had before we entered,
and some "offered up" their backaches resulting from sagging
mattresses. But were we not told in advance that we were coming to the missions? Some may have even been disappointed
that they didn't have straw mattresses on a floor. Adjusting to
the spartan living conditions was less difficult for some than
dealing with the strain of insufficient resources to serve the
people to whom we were ministering.

Few may have expected to find a spouse when joining
VTMS (changed to Catholic Lay Mission Corps in 1962), but
each year several announced engagements, and a few left to enter the postulancy of some religious order. When I left in August of 1963 for graduate school at the University of Portland,
I had known my future spouse, Joan Penzenstadler, for a year,
but not well. We had worked in cities about eighty miles apart
and talked briefly during occasional weekend get-togethers of
the members. During the summer of 1963 and through sub-
sequent correspondence between Portland, Oregon, my
home, and Monterrey, Mexico, where she was assigned by
CLMC to teach English at a boys' orphanage, our relationship
grew. In June of 1964, we married.

Like gaseous clouds that form a new star, most persons
who drifted into the VTMS/CLMC sun burned more lumi-
nously when they spun out of its gravitational attraction. I felt
a new power, a creative force for doing good, because I found
the goodness within me (the Christ at my core). Equally important, I could feel that radiance, which I call the Spirit of the
Father and the Son, in the presence of another. I may not have
sensed it as clearly then as I do now, because I was too often
blinded by my closeness to the overwhelming source of light.
Only a few, I dare say, didn't burn more brightly upon leaving
the organization.

Although I left CLMC for graduate school, I never left the lay apostolate. Upon completion of my master's degree in May 1965, Joan and I worked that summer with four seminarians in a team ministry to migrant farmworkers in the Willamette Valley of Oregon. We lived in the migrant camps and picked fruits and vegetables with them so that we could better know them and they could identify us with the Church—the four rural parishes that we represented. Without the presence of Joan and her fluency in Spanish, I would never have begun a ministry to and with the Mexican American population that continues to this day (my previous work with VTMS/CLMC as a teacher touched only a few Hispanics enrolled in the parochial school). Most of the time I was a silent partner when we talked with the Spanish-speaking migrants.

As a result of our summer contacts with agencies serving the migrants, I landed a job with the Willamette Valley Migrant League. That gave me an opportunity to serve both Hispanic and Anglo seasonal farm workers, initially as an adult education supervisor and later as a job counselor. Through two and a half years with VML, Joan and I were regularly involved with the Church. She eventually became a full-time English teacher at the major seminary for the Archdiocese of Portland.

When Fr. Underwood called me from Austin, Texas, in the spring of 1968, to become principal of his parochial school, Dolores (Nuestra Señora de Dolores), I felt that with my M.Ed. in school administration and my experience with Spanish-speaking migrants I was better qualified than I had ever been for anything I did in CLMC. As the first lay principal of the school, and one of only two lay administrators in the diocesan schools, I was very visible and a sign of the rapid changes occurring in the Church at that time. The parishioners were quick to acknowledge that a lay person could assume a Church leadership role previously reserved for a vowed religious person. It was more difficult for the bishop and his priest superintendent of schools who didn't have a high opinion of CLMC members because of various encounters with them throughout their respective administrations.

I would never have survived the four years as principal of Dolores School without the contributions of my wife. At times she went to work to supplement my salary—$3,600 a year initially, and gradually raised to $6,000. Just as significant was her contribution in developing curriculum, procuring human and material resources from the community, and training teachers. At other times she assisted me in the preparation of lessons or in the actual instruction of students that I taught on a part-time basis as principal. At the same time she nurtured our two children, age two and newly born when I began at Dolores. Like other CLMC colleagues before us at that school, we moved into low-income housing near the church. We could afford no other, and our family found identity with the Chicano community much easier when we shared their poverty, their problems with inadequate street drainage, trash and junk cars, etc. Acceptance of our lowered income and status was more difficult for our parents and relatives "up north" than for us.

During my fourth year as principal, I decided that, at age forty, I'd better find an income to provide for our children's education and our retirement. To say that God intervened would be a pious cliché. My plans to work with a community development project didn't materialize when federal funds didn't come through, and late August was a poor time to apply for an administrative or teaching job in the competitive Austin area. One day, during a visit to my confessor, I met a young man who had just returned from a year of volunteer service in New Mexico. During our conversation I suddenly recalled my memo, written in 1970 to the Texas Catholic Conference, outlining briefly a volunteer service program similar to CLMC which had folded in 1969. I announced to the young man, who had no cause to be interested in the TCC, that I would present my proposal to them again without delay. After several meetings with the TCC staff and a presentation to their board of directors (the bishops of Texas and other clergy and elected laity) I obtained their approval and a $4,000 seed grant to Volunteers for Educational Services. Thus a lay-funded organization was launched that eventually recruited, trained and placed qualified lay professionals in over one hundred ministries of education, social and medical services throughout Texas and parts of New Mexico. It became known as VESS, Volunteers for Educational and Social Services in 1975, when social services were added to the ministries.

From 1972 until I left the director's position in 1982, I witnessed the coming and going of about four hundred lay persons. They came from all over the United States and a few foreign countries. Unlike CLMC members, some VESS persons (at times as many as twenty-five percent) were of other Christian denominations. Most were trained for and/or experienced in the field they entered as VESS members; most had bachelor's degrees, some had master's degrees, and a few had Ph.D's. But all got equal stipends, food allowances and other benefits, except after the first year of service when the stipend increased $10 a month to provide for needs left unmet during their first year. Like CLMC members, most of them lived in households of two or more, pooling their food allowance, sharing household tasks and getting to know the other members whom they had no choice in selecting. Their choices were VESS, their ministry and the worksite, but not necessarily in that order. Most were strangers in a strange land. But a good number settled deep in the heart of Texas, after they experienced the welcoming abrazo of the people.

Texas' heat and innumerable insects did in some newcomers. But most were warned and expected to come to "missionary" country, and usually adjusted to the physical

discomforts and conditions of living among the poor served by
VESS. For some, the biggest problem was coping with their
supervisor, often a vowed religious, or their housemates. Living and working with a "stranger" whose habits and idiosyn-
cracies soon became known sometimes resulted in
confrontation and compromise. Many hours of my time as
VESS director were spent listening to their problems and ar-
bitrating conflicts within a household or with a supervisor.
Often I felt that my prayers and efforts to reconcile the parties
were efficacious. At other times I left them as broken as before, and feeling broken myself. Nevertheless, Christian community was always the ideal to strive for. Sin and selfishness
prevented us from achieving it.

Where I may have felt frustrated in reconciling dissatis-
fied VESS members, I experienced a healing and holiness
among them during our "Weekends of Renewal." A former
member described them as "celebrations of life . . . at which
the circle of worship, songs, hugs, clapping and more said that
we supported each other, had common goals and believed in
our work caring for others. We all had different positions, different reasons for being part of VESS, yet there was a common bond between us that clicked when the group came
together."

VESS is a story of numerous people being called to leave
their homelands for unknown territory, because most (eighty
to ninety) percent came from outside Texas. Whatever
prompted them to begin the journey, the pilgrimage changed
them. My privilege was to be God's instrument calling them to
the land of oil and cattle where they were to find Yahweh in
their midst.

To paraphrase the Gospel, I found more joy when one
VESS member discovered some Gospel value than in ninety-
nine who joined feeling no need to change. I believe, however,
that most were looking for change, but found it differently

than expected. While I also sought to effect change in members, in the process I too went through a transition, often similar to those above.

This tribute to the salvific power of Jesus Christ to transform lives, by responding to the Church's call to witness Christ to the world by word and action, would be incomplete without my sharing how the hierarchy and their supporting structure, the Texas Catholic Conference, assisted me during the ten year period of my ministry with VESS. Quite obviously, VESS would never have been launched without the vision and support of the bishops of Texas and the TCC staff. But beyond that initial stage, it demanded their continual review, their financial and moral support. The previous [deceased] archbishop of San Antonio, Francis Furey, readily lent his signature to grant proposals for VESS, concelebrated the Mass and shared the last supper at several annual orientations for VESS members. The present archbishop, Patricio Flores, has continued to be that visible sign of the magisterium to VESS members in additional ways: writing for the *VESS Parable* tabloid, presiding at banquets honoring them for their service and other less formal contacts that he and other bishops of Texas have with them when visiting parishes and other institutions of their diocese. The main liaison between VESS and the bishops continues to be Fr. Walter Dalton, C.S.P., co-director since 1974, whose credibility and wisdom helps open chancery doors and the treasuries of foundations.

Without the prompting and occasional prodding of John McCarthy, presently auxiliary bishop of Galveston-Houston and previously executive director of the TCC, VESS would be short an "S" and many ministries that resulted when social services were added in 1975. He was more than a boss during our five years of working together. Sometimes he was a confidant, often a protagonist and occasionally an antagonist, but always he was a friend. The same could be said for Fr. Dalton.

I share a special kinship in Christ with many vowed religious, especially those priests and sisters of worksites that VESS helped to staff. They often sustained the VESS members once they arrived from home or college and the orientation. If the VESS member's ego got beaten down by some sense of failure, they sometimes added the balm of encouragement, or recognized the need for someone else to do it. How often we shared our concern and challenged our wits to find ways of resolving adjustment problems or improving professional skills of some VESS member. Such labors together gave birth to building friendships and the Kingdom of God.

The Kingdom of God on earth, the Church, obviously has flaws. But how can its mission to preach the Gospel be accomplished with inadequately prepared lay apostles? Compare a week of orientation and four Weekends of Renewal for VESS members with the preparation a vowed religious gets before setting out to minister. Although Maryknoll gives its lay missionaries four months of training before departing to a foreign land, domestic lay volunteer organizations provide no more preparation than VESS does. How can lay ministers be expected to understand the calling to and meaning of discipleship with such a short preparation? Jesus spent three years with his disciples readying them for challenges to the Kingdom. Laity who are to give their services to the Church, either permanently or for a period of time, need a training equivalent to that given to vowed religious in Scripture, theology and Church history, in order to be credible representatives of the Church. Since the Church recognizes the decline of vowed religious vocations and the increased dependence on lay ministers, there should be a corresponding reallocation of resources to prepare these laity for discipleship.

Arthur J. Laffin

Ministering for Peace

If someone were to have told me ten years ago that I would become involved in a ministry of peacemaking, I never would have believed it. Although I had no clear career plans when I finished college, I knew that I wanted to serve God. In the years since then, my life has changed dramatically. I never imagined myself to be a speaker, writer, demonstrator or prisoner. But what I never once dreamed of doing has now become the central work of my life. In this article I will offer a reflection on my ministry. I will focus on key experiences that led me into peace work, my understanding of Christian ministry, what my ministry involves and how I am sustained in this work.

KEY FAITH EXPERIENCES

I began my journey of peacemaking when, following my graduation from the University of Prince Edward Island in Canada in 1976, I attended a Catholic Peace Fellowship Conference. Although my parents taught me at a young age the value of peacemaking, I never made it a priority. And even though I had read articles about the resistance to the Vietnam War and the peace movement prior to that time, I was quite oblivious to the fact that I had a responsibility to be a peacemaker. For the first time I met Christians who were actively involved in opposing the Vietnam War. These people of faith were honestly struggling to understand what their response should be to a nation and world marred with violence, poverty, racism, sexism and nuclear weapons. Their witness moved me to enter the same struggle.

I went from this conference to a job in Holland as a player-coach on a basketball team. The conference had opened my eyes and heart to a whole new world and I knew that I would never be the same. This marked the beginning of my journey through the wilderness, from a secure job to an adventure in faith. When I was not involved with my work, I was reading books by James Douglass, Dorothy Day, Thomas Merton, the Berrigans, Jean Vanier, Henri Nouwen, Martin Luther King and others on Christian pacifism, non-violent resistance, spirituality and social justice. The more I read about their unique journeys of faith, the more I hungered to know the reference point of their lives: Jesus.

After seven months in Holland, I resigned from my job and set out on a four-month pilgrimage to revitalize my then-dormant faith. I lived for a time in France at L'Arche, a community dedicated to working with the mentally handicapped, and visited Taizé and several other Christian communities committed to living out the Beatitudes. I attended an International Fellowship of Reconciliation conference in England where I met many long-time Christian peace activists.

While in England I was invited to attend an international conference on non-violence, peace and human rights in Londonderry, Northern Ireland sponsored by Pax Christi. This proved to be another turning point in my pilgrimage. As I prepared for this trip, I felt increasingly fearful. Having read about the extensive violence there, I began to wonder about my safety and whether I should go. My prayers led me to let go of my fear, place my trust in God and make the trip.

Journeying into this unfamiliar war-torn area was a test of

my faith. As we entered Northern Ireland, our bus was stopped and searched by heavily-armed British soldiers. Traveling farther, we passed through numerous military checkpoints. In Londonderry I saw countless sections of the city which had been bombed out. British soldiers patrolled the streets. The expressions on people's faces showed suspicion and despair, especially the youth. I felt afraid and wondered what I was doing there.

At the conference center, however, I was welcomed by several local people who quickly made me feel at home. I met other Christians from around the world whose stories of faith and struggle caused my own fear to subside. My faith and trust in God became rekindled. I was amazed at the hope I saw exhibited within both local and international participants, even in the midst of this civil-war zone. I was particularly privileged to meet and speak with Dom Helder Camara from Brazil, a man who has given his life to the poor and in non-violent witness for peace and justice. He confirmed my growing belief that non-violence is the true way to peace, even in Northern Ireland.

I left Northern Ireland with a greater faith in God who protected me during this difficult trip, enabling me to meet such hope-filled Christians, and a burning desire to commit myself to the Gospel of Jesus and to work for world peace.

After prayerfully reflecting on my four-month pilgrimage in Europe, I chose to relinquish my plans to pursue a promising sports career. I began to open my life up to the will of God and sought guidance. This discernment led me to return to my home state of Connecticut, where I would enflesh my newfound faith and commitment to work for peace.

Between 1977 and 1979 a number of experiences played a paramount role in determining the direction of my ministry. These included vigils for peace at the Pentagon in Washington, D.C. and General Dynamics' Electric Boat Division

(E.B.) in Groton, Connecticut (home of the first-strike Trident submarine), a thirty-seven-day fast for disarmament during the first United Nations Special Session on Disarmament, meeting survivors of the Hiroshima bombings who attended the session, studying Church teachings on war and peace, and conferring with many experts on the moral, medical, political, economic and environmental consequences of the nuclear threat.

One of the most powerful of these experiences was the first time I saw a Trident submarine. It was Thanksgiving Day, 1977. Instead of being filled with thanks on this holiday, my heart was full of anguish. As I vigiled at E.B. with some friends, I wondered how humans could create a weapon two football fields long and five stories high with the capability to unleash 408 individually-targeted warheads, each with a blast of five Hiroshima-sized bombs. I thought of how the workers' talents and the earth's precious resources were being need-lessly wasted by building a weapon capable of destroying millions of God's children. And this Trident before me was to be one of thirty planned by the navy! Gradually I became convinced that the only way to stop Trident and the nuclear-arms race is if people convert their lives to Christ's way of peace and non-violence.

I also felt a growing desire and need to be connected to Christians who, like me, were seeking to respond to the nuclear sin. I realized that if I were to be spiritually sustained in my ministry, I needed to be part of a community that would nurture my faith. Due to the enormity of the nuclear threat, I could not possibly see myself going on without this kind of community support.

I therefore moved from my home in Hartford to New Haven, where three friends and I began to explore the formation of a Christian peace community. In the spring of 1979, after nine months of prayerful discernment and working together on various peace efforts, we formed the Covenant Peace Community (CPC).

Since its inception, we viewed our community to be what Gandhi called an "experiment in truth." Our life together centered on the Gospel and daily communal prayer, through which we have continuously sought the Spirit's guidance to discern our future direction. We developed a peace ministry which involved speaking to Christian groups and participating in acts of non-violent direct action for peace. We chose to be a provisional community in that we attempted to lead a simple lifestyle in solidarity with the poor. We generated only enough income (through part-time work and donations) to meet basic needs.

Our "experiment in truth" has undergone great changes after four years. During the last year, after much prayerful reflection, we have come to see that we are being called in several directions and that each needs to follow his or her own calling. Although we are no longer together as an intentional community, we continue to maintain our friendships and remain committed to the work of peace and justice.

Sharing life with others day-to-day has often been a struggle. I have had to learn to serve rather than be served. I have had to put the needs of others before my own. With the love and support of brothers and sisters, I have begun to empty myself of individualism. As I serve others, Christ reveals himself to me, and I continue to hear his call to witness and minister in his name.

PEACE EVANGELIZATION AND NON-VIOLENT WITNESS

My ministry of peacemaking has been, and continues to be, an attempt to make visible Christ's message of unconditional love to a state and nation which is so heavily involved in preparing conventional and nuclear armaments that are capable of annihilating all life. This ministry has included peace-evangelization in churches, proclaiming the Gospel of peace, and participating in acts of non-violent witness for nuclear disarmament.

I have done speaking and preaching to many types of church groups—to parish groups, religious communities and young adult groups. I have met many who are questioning and hungering to find a relationship between their faith and the nuclear threat. In an attempt to respond to these questions of faith and conscience, three of us in the CPC were led to co-author a Gospel-based study book on the nuclear arms race entitled *The Risk of the Cross* (by Arthur Laffin, Elin Schade and Chris Grannis, New York, Seabury Press, 1981). To explore the meaning of Christian discipleship in the nuclear age, we used St. Mark's Gospel as the basis for our study. Written from a context of prayer, reflection, action and community, the hope of this book has been to enhance the development of groups focused on prayer, study and action. We believe that such groups are vital if peacemaking is to become a central priority in churches. We are thankful that our book has been one of many which have helped foster a growing consciousness of non-violence and peacemaking among Christians.

A second vital dimension of my ministry is a public non-violent witness for peace which includes vigils, fasts, distributing leaflets, and acts of civil disobedience. These witnesses become a natural extension of my faith, prayer, study and reflection. They are symbolic acts of repentance and hope through which the Gospel message of peace and love is communicated. A growing number of these witnesses are occurring at nuclear weapons research, production and storage centers throughout the United States, Canada, Western and Eastern Europe, the South Pacific, Japan and elsewhere. They have become channels for God's peace to transform those who participate as well as those who observe.

One act of public witness which I was recently involved in, the "Trident Nein" witness, serves to highlight this aspect of my ministry. Early on the morning of July 5, 1982, eight friends and I (all affiliated with the Atlantic Life Community—a network of East Coast spiritually-based resistance communities involved in non-violent campaigns at centers of warmaking) went to Electric Boat to begin the process of dismantling a Trident submarine, the USS Florida. In light of our government's failure to initiate any genuine disarmament after thirty-seven years and some six thousand talks, we felt morally compelled to perform this non-violent act of disarmament. We used symbols of blood paint and hammers to carry out our act. With blood and paint we renamed the submarine "USS Auschwitz" because of the holocaust it could potentially inflict on the world. The blood also symbolized those who die daily from hunger and disease because money, which might help them, is instead used to build such weapons systems (according to United Nations estimates, over fifty thousand children die each day from hunger, and nearly one billion live in dire poverty). We used hammers—simple carpenter's tools—on the submarine's missile hatches and sonar devices to enflesh the biblical mandate "to hammer swords into plowshares" and to prevent their ever being used to kill a human being. Together we awaited arrest, offering readings from the Scriptures and prayers for peace. We underwent trial in New London, Connecticut and were convicted by a somewhat sympathetic jury on two felony counts and a misdemeanor. We served sentences ranging from six months to one year as a consequence of our conviction.

We went to Electric Boat because we believe that Trident is anti-God and anti-life; it has no more right to exist than the Nazi gas ovens did. The real crime here is not our hammering on the Trident, but rather our government's and Electric Boat's deliberately preparing for mass murder. Despite the fact that we have been convicted and jailed for our actions, I believe that we are innocent under both divine and international law.

My preparation for this witness involved a rigorous, prayerful examination of conscience in which I was confronted by great fears and guilt. I feared the prospect of a long prison term: separation from family and friends, relinquishing familiar activities and joys, and discarding future plans.

I saw how my earlier years of silence and indifference made me guilty of complicity in our nation's sinful nuclear war preparations. Through my prayer and with the spiritual support of a loving community of friends, I was able to move beyond my own fears and guilt to trust and obedience. The closer I came to discerning God's will for me, the less preoccupied I was about my fears and anxieties. I remembered the words of Jesus: "Fear is useless; what is needed is trust" (Mk 5:6). I realized that I could do nothing more important than follow God's will, even if it meant the wilderness of jail. In this realization and with the encouragement of my family, community and brother and sister prisoners, I found the inner peace and empowerment to sustain me through my six months in jail.

HOPE AND NOURISHMENT

My work for peace has been very life-giving, but also very difficult. Increasingly, though, my fears and difficulties have given way to a renewed belief in the promise of new life and freedom that Christ has gained for all humanity through his cross and resurrection. I truly believe that if Christians place their trust in God and follow Christ's ethic of love, the powers of this world—the power of the bomb—will not prevail. However, to accept Jesus' invitation to experience and make visible the power of love also implies a risk. Christ's love for the world took him to the cross. We, too, must prepare for similar sacrifice. I have learned that each time I am called to take such a risk, I am carried through by God's grace.

Jesus offers to us the bread and wine of the Eucharist to prepare us for the journey ahead. These are symbols of his life poured out in love, and an assurance that he will always sustain us throughout the hardships we will encounter on our journey. The Eucharist serves as both a source of spiritual nourishment which sustains our lives and a constant reminder of each Christian's call to be committed to the way of the cross and to the hope of the resurrection.

I am confident that all who struggle to minister for Christ will be led through the wilderness of our time. My journey of peacemaking has been, and continues to be, a wilderness experience. At times I have often felt unsure of my direction and overwhelmed. During these moments of uncertainty, I have turned to God. Through the power of prayer and community I have gained clarity for my life. Each time I act in faith, Christ is revealed to me. By God's grace my life has become a vehicle for the ministry of Christ. I give thanks to God for showing me what it means to minister in Christ's name.

Patricia O'Connell Killen

Lay Ministry:
School of Discipleship

When I was growing up, my mother responded to my very definite pronouncements of what I would and would not do with the phrase: "Don't make positive statements." Then I went off to a Jesuit college, became a religious studies major and made very strong pronouncements about how I would never be a director of religious education or pastoral associate, vocations to which many of my fellow theology majors aspired. I intended to teach theology to undergraduates.

The day I returned home from burying my mother, there was a letter on my desk from the bishop of Nashville appointing me "lay minister with immediate responsibility for coordinating the activities" of the Sewanee Catholic Community. My mother had been right: positive statements often provide the occasion to laugh at oneself. But the laughter is a gift, for it opens us up to seeing the often missed invitations from God which lie all around us. My specific lay ministry—as the designated leader for the Sewanee Catholic Community—is best summarized as a continuous invitation from God to love and to be at home in creation. Finally, I think that any ministry is a school of discipleship.

Before elaborating on this theme, some background on the Sewanee Catholic Community is in order. My ministry has been without question part of a communal venture. The permanent community members, never more than eleven households and now down to six, have all given of their own time and energy, as have the students who cared enough about their faith to be active. It has been an honor for me to be in a leadership position with this group.

The Sewanee Catholic community began four years ago as an experimental association of Catholics on a small rural university campus on the edge of the Cumberland Plateau, ninety miles southeast of Nashville. There is only one priest for the three counties that converge here. The Catholic faculty and staff and the Catholic members of the Sewanee Catholic Community (population 1,500 without students) realized that we would have to be church for each other and for the one hundred or so Catholic college students at the University of the South (an Episcopalian institution) if we were going to grow in our faith. The situation called us to a more mature living out of our baptismal promises. It also presented us with a distinctive purpose: to enable young adults to develop the skills and understanding necessary for effective participation in priestless parishes. They leave here to be part of a Church where our situation is increasingly the norm and not the exception.

With the approval of Bishop Niedergeses, we organized our Catholic community. It has been a "learn-as-you-go" operation. Of the original eight persons on the steering committee, two of us had graduate degrees in theology. (My full-time occupation is teaching in the School of Theology at the University of the South.) Many of us had experience in community organizations. All of us had full-time jobs and families.

We organized the community with offices and committees, designing them to provide the three basic activities of any Christian community: worship, proclamation, and service. As much as possible we have operated with shared leadership. Most of the community's decisions are made by an executive

committee chaired by the president and made up of officers
and committee chairpersons. The practical necessity of
spreading the work around in this all-volunteer community
has helped us to maintain shared leadership.

As the lay minister for a priestless community, I occupy a
role with which Catholics, including myself, have had little experience and for which we have received little preparation.
Lay ministry in a parish with a full-time resident pastor is one
thing; ministry by a community of laity is quite another. The
last four years' experience has been a school of discipleship for
me. In practical terms I have had to balance the community's
goal of shared leadership with the charge I received from the
bishop. This has required judgment, restraint, and discernment on my part. I have also been forced to reflect on the
meaning of this role for the community and for myself. I have
looked to models and images from the tradition for guidance.

The documents of Vatican II make it clear that all baptized Catholics share in the priestly, kingly, and prophetic
ministry of Jesus.[1] These images, as intended and understood
in those documents, tend not to be those evoked in the minds
of most American Catholics when they hear the words. As a
married laywoman, the image of priest has not been a particularly comfortable or useful one for me or for the community.
To view the lay leader of a priestless parish as a "little" or
"lesser" priest does not, I think, enhance the community's
sense of identity, esteem, or responsibility for ministry. Being
female and American, the concept of king was not much help
either. The image of prophet covers some aspects of my ministry, e.g., calling volunteers to account when they fail to meet
their commitments, and speaking the truth about the strengths
and weaknesses of the community. That image by itself, however, is still too limited.

The model that has helped me most to understand and to
define my role is that of the Hebrew sage from the Wisdom lit-

erature.[2] I think that the image aptly describes the role of non-ordained heads of Catholic communities at a time in the Church when normative thinking still dictates an ordained person as the center and head.

The Hebrew sage was not ordained or ritually confirmed in a position within the community. Sages gained authority by their ability to read human experience and to present the image of God in creation. The sage was a person characterized by openness to the world, a person who appreciated, valued, and enjoyed life. The sage operated at the margin of structural authority.[3]

All of this has been true of my experience. My ministry has involved training and supporting the officers and committee chairpersons, creating the basic organizational structure of the community, serving as the center of communication within the community and between the diocese and the community, helping to plan and organize the major liturgies, doing sacramental preparation, providing or recruiting resources for educational events, giving spiritual direction, acting as the theological resource person, recruiting priests to celebrate the Eucharist, being with people in times of death or crisis, and standing as the reminder, the prodder, the vision-keeper.

Accomplishing these tasks effectively has depended on my openness and honesty, my ability to speak truths that need saying, not from a position of formal authority but from a position of clear perspective. It has required presence, love, and action kept separate from ego-demanding expectations. It has required committed involvement from me as a person, not involvement authorized by occupying a clearly defined office. The more I read about Hebrew sages, men and women, the more I think that my ministry parallels theirs. For the present, Wisdom and God's presence in human experience support and sustain me in this pioneering role. For the future, a different model appropriate to this ministry may evolve from the cur-

rent debate over the structural and sacramental issues surrounding priestless Catholic communities.

I accepted and serve in the ministry of being a designated
leader in a Catholic community with no resident priest because
I was called upon by the bishop and the community to do so.
My educational background coupled with my gifts for organization and facilitation enabled me to respond to the call. I have
found the role to be rewarding and costly, satisfying and vex-
ing. Over the last four years I have experienced the warmth of
joy and the chill of anxiety about my ministry. Through it all,
however, God has beckoned me onward. Awareness of God's
constant invitation to love and hospitality has been the center-
ing thread for my ministry.

What have been the costs? The time and energy involved
have been larger than I ever expected. This ministry has
slowed my professional academic development. I have neither
written as many articles nor read as many books as I intended
because of it. Further, this ministry has added to the strains
that occur naturally in a two-career marriage. Finally, there
have been the frustrations of being involved in a pioneering effort, the doubts that accompany weariness, when one longs to
see the fruits of her labor and none are apparent.

Beyond the fact of having been called to this ministry,
and in spite of the costs, I am engaged in it because I believe
that I am called as a baptized Catholic Christian to be a center
of God's love and presence wherever I am. Further, I believe
that this central call can be concretized or embodied only
through involvement in some ministry to which one is committed. Thus, a specific lay ministry becomes the school of
discipleship within which one is molded, strengthened, and
challenged.

The educators in my school of discipleship have been people, joyful events, and difficult times. The priests who have
helped the Sewanee Catholic Community over the last four

years have persistently called on all of us to be mature in our faith, to support each other. Their call has come through word and deed as they have celebrated the Eucharist for us and provided the other sacraments, often at great inconvenience to themselves. They have challenged us to be a worshiping community through liturgy of the word with Communion even when we cannot have a priest.

Each member of the community has shown me something about who I am and how I follow Christ. Often they do not know that they are inviting me to notice, that they are my teachers. One Saturday afternoon the bread-baker for that month had forgotten to bring the bread. She had to return home, get it out of her freezer, take it by her neighbor's house to thaw in the microwave, and get back to the chapel before the offertory. She was embarrassed and upset. At first I was angry, then self-pitying about my lot with this community, and finally, moved to laughter at my foolishness. That incident was a critical lesson for me in trust and responsibility. Ultimately it freed me from unnecessary fear and anxiety by initiating a reflection on my need to have everything "under control."

My education in discipleship has come through joyful times. These have included Mass, the yearly visit from Bishop Niedergeses, blessing of unborn babies in the community, commissioning of eucharistic ministers, First Communions, baptisms, confirmations, parties, and potlucks. In all of these and more, I have been invited to love and to be at home in God's creation. In all of them I experience delight in creativity and joy in having nurtured and taught many of the people and projects involved. Hearing graduating student members of the community say that they intend to be practicing adult Catholics as a result of their involvement in the Sewanee Catholic Community brings me great joy.

The hard times have included conflict, which is always

painful in a small community, the refusal of students to accept liturgies of the word with Communion services, the attitude, less prevalent now than in the past, of "if only we had a priest who would take care of us," the pain of being with someone as a spouse dies, and the reality of all the things I want to do for the community and cannot because of the limitations of time and my own personal limitations. These hard times provide the same invitations to notice and to reflect as do the joyful times.

The people, the joyful times, and the hard times are all invitations of love and hospitality from God, invitations to notice who I am and how I am in the world. They are invitations to love without counting the costs and without demanding results. Through my ministry I have grown in wisdom and love and willingness to suffer as a follower of Christ. Though I had said yes to these before, comprehending the full dimensions of that "yes" required my being fully committed to a lay ministry. There is no question that committed ministry involves suffering and joy, that the invitation to discipleship is a call to know and to befriend both.

I do not know what will happen to the Sewanee Catholic Community in the future. We have designated this year as a time of prayerful self-assessment. We sense a shift, a period of transition in our life as a community.

I can identify clearly three things that have come to me over the last four years. Through my involvement with the Sewanee Catholic Community I have been taught to see, taught to keep myself in perspective, and taught that ministry is finally God's work and not mine. Vision, perspective, and faith have been the transforming lessons for me in this school of discipleship. The transformation of the minister lies at the heart of any person's call to ministry.

[This article first appeared in *Rural Roots*, the bimonthly magazine of the Rural Ministry Institute.]

NOTES

1. Vatican Council II, *Decree on the Apostolate of the Laity*, chapter 1, n.2; *Decree on the Ministry and Life of Priests*, chapter 1, n.2.

2. This model was first suggested to me by friend Arthur E. Zannoni, Ph.D., theologian-in-residence at St. Thomas Aquinas Center, the Catholic Center at Purdue University, West Lafayette, Indiana.

3. See Arthur E. Zannoni, "The Hebrew Sage: A Model for Lay Campus Ministry," *Process*, Volume 4, No. 2, Spring 1978, pp. 9–12; "Five Disconcerting Theological Reflections from Old Testament Wisdom Literature," *St. Luke's Journal of Theology*, Volume 19, No. 4, pp. 286–298.

Experiences of a Lay Minister: Uncertainties, Contrasts, Hopes

"When you've graduated with your M.B.A., will you get a 'real job'?" was the question asked of me several months ago in a conversation with a friend about my future plans. It has echoed around in me many times since then and in some strange way captures what I have come to recognize as the reality of those of us who call ourselves "lay ministers." We are a new experience in the Church—one which I don't believe that the Church, as a whole, has yet come to understand or, in some more severe circumstances, acknowledges as even valid or needed.

My experiences of the past fifteen years as a laywoman without religious vows, working full-time in the Church, have been filled with similar questions. These questions have risen out of the uncertainties, contrasts and hopes generated by the myriad of experiences, my reflections on them and both the re-solved and unresolved realities discovered in them. I want to share some of these in this brief article, both to challenge the Church and to encourage other lay ministers.

I believe that a word common to all my different situa-tions, ministries, projects and efforts is uncertainty. Even now, in my role of archdiocesan administration, I would never assume that my life is stable and certain, because in reality my ministry even here is contingent on the presence of the current archbishop and his leadership and/or the fiscal stability of the archdiocese. That is to say, if in either case a major change would occur, I might very easily find myself without a "job," not unlike any parish ministers whether they are DRE's, youth ministers or young adult ministers who often find themselves terminated with the change of pastor or when the parish council cuts budgets. This, of course, is in stark contrast to the ordained and vowed ministers who will always have a location for their ministerial work, "a job."

Because we are not, for the most part, recognized by the Church (and here I am not speaking of clergy, but laity as well) we are expendable. It is this reality that motivated the question in my first paragraph. Why would anyone deliberately choose to stay in such an uncertain situation if other more stable choices existed? It is still confusing and bewildering for most Catholics to acknowledge the possibility that a lay person might choose a career in ministry. The thinking of the lay apostolate movement told us that ministry is something done by priests and sisters whereas lay people "volunteer" to help them.

My choices around all this have always been free and very deliberate. Upon leaving a religious community in the 1960's, I didn't leave to be "going away from," but rather to be "coming into." I experienced a growing realization that the ministry of full-time religious education was what I wanted. During a period of time, while on leave from the religious community I then belonged to, I worked in my home parish as a parish director of religious education. In this experience it became clear that I could be involved with a total parish community, be involved in the work I loved the most and be in a very real sense a minister to the people I worked with and for. This was encouraged and supported by some very significant people in my life, and so I made the decision to move in this direction as a career. There was no single overwhelming inspiration at this

time which motivated me other than the life experience I had
of "doing religious education ministry" and simultaneously
having the opportunity to invest myself in the life of a parish
community struggling in its own renewal and growth.

Since those years I have heard literally hundreds of similar stories from laywomen and men who have also had a taste
of ministry, been excited and energized by it and have then
made deliberate choices to prepare themselves and seek out opportunities to give their skills and enthusiasm to the Church.
This is not a new experience in the Church. It is one which
finds its roots in the calling of the Apostles and today is seen in
the women and men who live out religious and priestly lives.
Yet, in the majority of dioceses and parishes, these laymen and
women are not recognized, supported or nurtured in their vocation (a word incidently still not attached to their "calling").

I have come to experience this in myself and many others
as very closely connected with a perception of what Church is
and means. This reflection was not recognized quickly for me.
Rather, it has been a growing truth over several years. The reflection goes something like this. I chose a career in ministry
which I come to know as both my right and responsibility
flowing from the gift of my baptism and my full membership
in the Church. This baptismal call is supported by my gifts of
personal faith and the willingness to struggle with my failings
and uncertainties, my ability to teach and lead others, my love
for the Church and its people. The best place I can live out all
this and respond to what I have come to know in so many ways
as my vocation is by a full-time career of ministry in the
Church. The community on its side has accepted, that is,
"hired" me, and it validates my ministry explicitly through my
salary and benefits and implicitly through the fact that I have
been given responsibilities to carry out and a certain credibility
currently through the archbishop and before that through various pastors.

A comment here might be that there are some strong parallels between this experience and that of vocation as sacramentalized in holy orders. The major difference is, of course, the lack of explicit recognition by the Church of this ministry other than compensation. Recognition is not a matter of status as much as it is a matter of naming. Families, organizations, communities name the functions within them in order to better enable successful interaction and relationships. Lay ministry is one of those functions which, for the most part, has had to name itself.

I am growing in my realization that this has a very significant influence on the tensions of stablizing the role of lay ministers, their relationship with the Church community and other ministers, and their own personal belief in themselves and their self-worth—all of which are related to levels of motivation and commitment.

To return briefly to the original point concerned with the baptismal call and membership in the community, it seems to me that as our ecclesiology moves from the "layered-pyramid" to the "inter-active-circle," lay ministry will become less needful of recognition because other ministries will also become less concerned with public recognition. Community will hopefully mean full integration of all members and not a leadership which to some degree is apart from or even over and above. A book which I have returned to many times for encouragement and challenge along these lines, *Building Christian Communities*, refers to this possibility as "holistic" community. What I am suggesting, in the meantime, is some visible acknowledgement by the Church of the emerging reality of its *new vocations*, its lay ministers. This naming of ministry is for me directly connected with the realities of stability and continuity in my ministry. It seems to me that as my ministry is recognized and supported, I will, in turn, be more free to give my gifts to the community as well as to receive theirs. The bonding of community will be more than in word only. I experienced this in a real way in my first years in the Archdiocesan Office of Religious Education. This was a period of extremely limited financial support and very little general affirmation by the people we served. The 1970's were years of severe resistance by those who thought that religious education was being taken over by radicals and liberals, a little less than heretics. Those of us on the archdiocesan staff, along with a majority of the parish DRE's, formed an organization which sustained our energy and vision. This group enabled many of us to find a way to "stay alive" in the ministry of our choice and to work toward a fuller experience of what it meant to be Church. It became a means of motivation toward a lifestyle from which our ministries drew energy.

No one whom I have worked with in those years or even now came to lay ministry with the personal goal of becoming wealthy. Rather, I would say that I am more typical of the persons who have come with a goal of being able to carry out a response of faith through career ministry with at least a sense of stability and reasonable security. It is difficult to discuss with most lay ministers, including myself, the notion of "simple lifestyle" when for all practical purposes it is not a choice. Rather, it is a reality, given us by our uncertainty, our limited resources and the ambiguity of our state.

Those in the tradition of the Church who have lived out a simple lifestyle have been supported in this witness by a community which values and encourages it. I learned a long time ago that I prefer the opportunity to choose this lifestyle and not have it imposed on me by others who do not value either my skills or the people that I work for and with. The lifestyle choices I continually make are ones that ensure my ability to continue to work in this way and simultaneously make some statement about the ideas and directions valuable to the community.

Another significant aspect of my ministry lifestyle is the fact that I am unmarried. I prefer the word unmarried over single, because I never think of myself as single. I have several very close friends who have been part of my life over the years of lay ministry and who are integral to who I am and, therefore, what I do. The closeness I have with them is another primary source of hope and energy for my ministry. I was into full-time lay ministry for less than a year when I realized the very real need I had for a small group of people with whom I might share hopes, dreams, successes and failures. I have had the wonderful gift of these friendships all along and I know without hesitation that they have played a significant role in my continuance.

Once again, this corresponds with the experiences shared with me by other lay ministers, married and unmarried. It seems that ministry is one of those life experiences that cannot be kept in a compartment, but must permeate all corners of life and be influenced by the total person. My experience does not support the theory that married ministers are less able to give of themselves freely to those they serve. On the contrary, what my experience does confirm is that ministers who are unable to form real, intimate and personal relationships with others have a greater probability of withdrawing from ministry totally or at least of hiding in some thing(s) where they feel their personal needs are met. I am not suggesting a simplistic either/or arrangement. We all struggle with choices. But what I am suggesting is that there seems to be some very real connection between healthy people and successful ministry.

Lifestyle, for me, is who I am and how that is acted out in the way I live my life. Like the earlier thoughts on holistic ecclesiology, a simple lifestyle for me is one that is struggling toward wholeness. Time, power, comfort, places or health won't own or control me. Rather, they are all good and part of my life and contribute to it for a good far greater than the sum of all their parts. My ministry is connected in a real way with my effort toward holiness or wholeness as a complete baptized laywoman, unmarried and wanting to bring my gifts to others and to receive theirs.

In thinking about all this, it is difficult to sort out whether some prior insights or learning contributed to my thinking or if my more immediate work experiences have given me the opportunity to see a larger picture in which all of the preceding is somehow framed. I once heard a talk by a national leader in religious education in which he described his experiences of life, Church and ministry as his "sand castle theology." That is, he saw the building up of new directions like the building of sand castles which stood shining in the sun only to crumble as the rays dried them and the waves moved in and washed them away, to be rebuilt again by others from the same sand, only to go and come back again. This talk stayed with me and bothers me even now, because again my experience has not been one of building destruction. Granted, there have been frustrations and disappointments, but there have also been marvelous signs of growth.

This experience of positive and negative direction is not like the contrast of light and dark or sun and rain. One has not always followed the other. Rather, there have been times when both have been present simultaneously in a very complete way.

This reality is possibly close to the notion of ancient Chinese philosophers who developed the concepts around "Yin-Yang." That is, all change is the result of the interaction between the darkness or shade (north side of a hill) and light (south side of a hill). It is like the inter-activity of positive and negative forces creating a new meaning.

For example, one of the high points for me as an archdiocesan director of religious education was when I had the privilege of giving the homily at the Religious Education Congress for the dioceses of Washington State. I was the first non-priest to do this and, needless to say, was both challenged and frightened by the opportunity. Even as I stood in front of the fifteen hundred participants, I was aware of the levels of frustration and confusion within me, that homilies by the laity were still not acceptable, that we were still having religious education congresses in which we focused our attention on children only and not of the faith development of the whole community, that there were women and men in that congregation, not unlike me, who wanted the opportunity to minister and that this was being denied. Would I prolong these errors by not addressing them in my remarks or would I in some way work toward meeting them by giving the homily on the readings in the best way I could?

In a sense, I am speaking to the tension and pain I've experienced over the last few years in archdiocesan leadership of trying to constantly sort out whether I am really working to change the problems or whether I am so much a part of the institution that I cannot always separate myself from the problems—another glimpse of that dark and light not really following each other but all present together. I could say that my situations have seemed much more like early spring days when the sky can be bright in sunlight and dotted with heavy storm clouds with rain coming down at the same time.

Another period of my ministry which was full of the contrasts was in the years as a parish DRE and then as an Archdiocesan Religious Education Office staff member. I was involved in forming the Archdiocesan Religious Educators Association (AREAS) and not long after that the program for Master Catechists and the Introduction to Ministries Program. In all of these efforts I experienced growth not only in the development of catechetical ministries, both salaried and volunteer, but in the deepening of the skills and proficiency with which this work was being done. Catechetics was moving toward a period of being valued and respected and supported in the vast majority of the parishes.

Woven into all this were still the dark threads of mistrust by people holding up Catholic schools as the only legitimate way of educating; of the myth that volunteers would always be enough and therefore compensation was limited and even discouraged; of lay ministers themselves who refused to take themselves seriously enough to grow in their faith and to develop the skills to share it more effectively.

These dark threads served to highlight some of the frustrations which are still a very real part of my ministry, but the successes have, in the meantime, deepened the bonding of the ministers who were part of them. I now experience more people modeling a positive way to meet the old needs and the new dreams.

Another set of contrasts stems from my experiences of starting what has become known as the Lay Ministers Association. Even here it was a terrible frustration that motivated me to begin. The archdiocese was in the process of developing its first set of archdiocesan goals. They were to be circulated for input among all the leadership groups of the archdiocese. When I received them, I had no way to receive reactions back from the several hundred lay ministers who I knew were involved in the Church's work. It so angered me that I invited a group of eight women lay ministers to meet with me to simply discuss what might be done to prevent a future problem such as this. This conversation led to a second gathering with an additional eight male lay ministers over a period of several months until we found that there was an eagerness to form a permanent group.

The day we met with the archbishop to tell him of our plans, he supported us totally and remarked, "It seems like something I should have done. I didn't, but I'm glad you did." This all sounds like the sunny day. Some of the storm clouds appear this way—some lay ministers who are frightened by the change and suspect a "union"; lay people who work for the Church but don't consider themselves as ministers, but rather employees and see the organization as a threat to their identity, security, etc.; laity and clergy alike who see it as a "anti-clerical" statement; members who joined thinking systemic change would come faster and left out of disappointment.

One final example of this pattern of contrasts might be my experience of the past two years during which I have served as the director of the Faith and Community Development Division for the archdiocese. This is a new configuration of agencies which includes what was formally known as the Offices of Religious Education, Worship, Campus and Young Adult Ministry, Catholic Youth, Hispanic Ministry, Missions and the Ecumenical and Interreligious Affairs Commission. It is all connected with the archbishop's goal of restructuring central services to better provide parishes and institutions with the needed resources. I have been given the responsibility of restructuring these agencies and their boards and of leading this group to its new position in the archdiocese. This responsibility both challenged and frightened me from the start. I accepted it as a sign of confidence on the part of the Church through the person of the archbishop. It also seemed to be a further statement of the Church's acknowledgement that laymen and women can and are willing to do these tasks. I made a choice and commitment to do the best job I could.

I saw it as an opportunity to make a statement about the role of lay ministers in the full life of the Church. The people I have worked with over the years support me in this and have continued to do so even up to the most difficult period in which some staff had to be terminated. The painful contrasts come to me in the realizations I have on a daily basis in my encounters with other lay ministers that even as I enjoy the support and confidence of Archbishop Hunthausen, they are not even allowed to participate in meetings of sub-deanery groups of priests around issues they work on in common; that our theological and pastoral education opportunities are still held in separate priest and non-priest groups; that there is an institutional isolationism preventing parishes from interacting either within the Church or ecumenically; that racism, sexism and clericalism are very much part of our institutional make-up and are creating layers of prejudice that make true growth slow and painful.

Yet, the light is there in a way that it allows me to see growth. My ministry has continued for some fifteen years and there are men and women working in the archdiocesan church who have been serving as long as I and who are still excited and motivated by successes and new hopes. Ministries are being called forth in new and unexpected ways and communities are supporting them to a greater and greater degree. The sharp angles of the pyramidal Church are being eroded by the renewal to the soft, inclusive arms of the circle.

I believe that this will continue, and not only at the current rate but in a proportionate increase as more and more experience the deep faithfulness of a Church which is a community of baptized and eucharized believers, served by people who have been called by the same community to share their talents and faith as enablers of other ministers. My experience is that as the Rite of Christian Initiation of Adults grows and has a chance to renew a parish, the value of many ministers is better recognized and named.

I also believe that this will cause lay ministers to come forth and act in a responsible and convicted way not only about what they do, but about who they are, their skills, competencies and proficiencies taking on new value to themselves and those to whom they minister. In a word, I suspect that they will take themselves more seriously and, in turn, be taken more seriously. I know from my own life that when I was valued and at the same time knew what I was capable of doing, it was then that I was able to step out with some confidence in myself and at the same time engender that in others.

Finally, so much of what I have done and learned in the rich years as a lay minister relates to the realization that I would have never been able to do it alone. All has been done with others. The current buzz word is networking. It is both my belief and my hope that lay people in ministry will see the value of connecting with each other formally and informally to be of support in every sense of that word.

My understanding of support is that there is someone to advise, encourage and lift me up, but that there is also someone who will help me recognize and do something with my weaknesses and failures. Blind approval has never been productive for me, and so much of my growth stems from the friend who offered positive criticism and constructive ways of changing. This type of networking or community connectedness, depending on your point of view, will strengthen the individuals as well as the vision.

The one nagging fear I have is not that we won't be recognized or valued or even that lay ministry will die. It is rather that as we struggle for our own identity and place we will fall victim and be entrapped by the frustrations and institutional limitations of which we are so critical. I am capable of being preoccupied about control, authority, power or structures for their own sake as much as anyone.

The model of "communidades de base" of the Hispanic peoples might better be the model for the Church of the future and, in that, the model for the future evolution of all ministries—an evolution to such a degree that all the angles of the triangle will have disappeared and all that will be left is a circle of people caring for each other.

H. Richard McCord

Lay Ministry:
A Personal Journey

There is a story told about a young man who entered a monastery. Very soon afterward he began to notice and be dismayed by the fact that monks, especially ones older than himself, were leaving the monastery. Troubled and confused, he went to the abbot. Why, he asked, do some men, after having committed themselves to a way of life, then forsake it for something else? The abbot responded with a story: Once upon a time a dog lay sleeping in the warm sun of the village square. All of a sudden, out of the corner of his half-opened eyes, he spied a rabbit darting across the road. He took off immediately in hot pursuit. He ran up and down the streets, through the countryside, keeping up the chase day and night and seeming never to tire. Eventually, other dogs saw him and joined in the run. But, one by one, they grew tired and stopped running. Why? They were running only because they had seen the first dog doing so. They had never caught sight of the rabbit in the first place. So, the abbot concluded, the one who has never glimpsed the vision easily grows tired of running. He gives up the chase because he can't remember why he had begun to run in the first place.

What sort of vision must be glimpsed initially if one is to run the course of lay ministry? My answer is tentative and, necessarily, incomplete. I've been running the race for a relatively short time. But, moreover, I think there are very few long track records. This is why I hope that whatever incidents and insights I'm able to share from my own experience will enrich our collective experience of lay ministry.

I have been a professional or career lay minister for more than ten years. I came to it, not unlike many of my contemporaries, almost directly from a seminary where I was close to concluding my studies for the priesthood. Due at least partly to these circumstances, I am aware of a certain continuous ministerial journey in my adult life. In other words, I cannot recall having been called to ministry, then having rejected it entirely, and then having been called all over again. Having chosen not to become a priest, I chose instead "a road less traveled." I chose to minister in and for the institutional Church as a layman. For me, the difference has nothing to do with ontological character, or special graces, or aspiring to a higher level of vocation. The difference is one of expression. I am expressing now as a layman (married and a father) the same basic call to ecclesial ministry that I felt over ten years ago and which had once propelled me toward priesthood.

The vision which I first glimpsed as a young man remains with me, at least in its essential shape, as I draw nearer to the middle years of adult life. That vision is all about giftedness. It is an experience of God's love embodied in other human beings, mediated through them to me, enabling me to sense my own lovableness and, from that center, to reach out in loving service. Now, lest this all seem too good to be true, let me hasten to add that this vision has had its peaks and valleys. Over the years it has been nuanced and rearticulated countless times. But its core is unchanged. What inspired me to want to be a lay minister is what led me to want to minister as an ordained priest. In time, I found that, although my call was to ministry, it was not to ordination. If I can keep attuned to the call, keep glimpsing the vision, I may find that my call to minister leads to the permanent diaconate. On the other hand, it may lead away from professional service in the institutional Church. I would even like to think, although it seems far-fetched, that my call could lead toward priesthood as a married man.

But, in the end, I don't think it matters what expression my call to ministry takes. The important thing is that I keep listening for the call and remain in possession of the vision. To stay in contact with the vision is to be hearing the call to minister. This vision of giftedness—God's gift in Jesus, the Lord's many gifts in his Spirit, my gifts placed at the service of others—is certainly not a static picture. As I develop and grow, so too does my consciousness of my gifts. I find, however, that to be conscious of a gift is not necessarily to accept it or to be willing to use it. For example, I'm aware that I have gifts of tenderness and compassion. I could use these in ministry but, very often, I don't. I retreat to a position of neutrality and rationality in relating to others. I'm not really sure why this occurs. But there is one thing I do know. What I cannot receive as gift I cannot give in ministry. The extent to which I block a gift is the extent to which the vision is dimmed. When the vision is dimmed, the call grows faint. Without a call there is no ministry.

What shape has my ministry in and for the Church taken? About a year after leaving the seminary I became director of religious education for a parish not too far from my home town. A year later I moved to a larger parish where I became one of two DRE's on staff there. During this period I also did some part-time work for the diocesan office. In another two years I found myself in a large northeastern city where I had come to join the diocesan staff as adult religious education consultant. Two years after that I was appointed director of the office and, a few years later, my responsibilities were expanded to include the direction of diocesan educational services for adult faith enrichment, parish renewal, evangelization, family ministry, permanent diaconate formation, and supervision of the diocesan liturgy office. All of these ministries translate into a staff of twenty-four full- and part-time persons including myself.

My academic preparation and general background have given me a strong foundation in education, particularly catechesis, and in management. Over the years it has always made sense to me to keep forging a link between them. At one time, particularly in the final years of my seminary studies, I wanted to pursue an academic career in Scripture and Semitic languages. But, after I left the seminary, it quickly became obvious that this would be a long and difficult road—one which I wasn't sure I could ask a wife and family to share with me. Even more particularly, I questioned whether I could support a family in this rather specialized academic field.

It was after I had taught some Bible classes at a parish that the pastor of another parish asked me to take over the direction of his religious education program, particularly concentrating on inservice to his catechists. This invitation set me on a track toward lay ministry in catechetics. Later, as I was taking some graduate courses in theology, I was invited by one of my classmates to become her associate on the religious education staff of a larger parish. I moved into diocesan level work in much the same way. A visiting professor from whom I was taking a summer course invited me to apply for a staff position in the adult religious education office which he directed.

As I look back over this brief history, I feel very fortunate to have been touched by certain persons. It was they who recognized my gifts and invited me to express them in different situations and roles of service. It was they who established a kind of mentor relationship in which I've been able to recognize and develop my gifts. This has helped me to stay in touch with the vision and the call.

As I look back, too, I can see that my path has taken me from a narrow field of education, to a broader form of education, to the very broad management of educational services. Right now I'd identify my lay ministry career as the management of ministerial education services.

This is a particularly satisfying place for me to be right now. For one thing, it puts me in the midst of a lot of creative ferment and new development in our Church today. Quite literally, none of the issues I deal with is encrusted with the dust of centuries. Most of them are post-Vatican II vintage. For example, I find myself in conversation with such matters as building small faith communities, enabling varieties of peer ministry, reaching out to alienated Catholics and sexual minorities, helping people to become self-directed learners, investigating the use of new communications technology for learning, and advocating for systemic changes that will encourage lay ministry. Because I'm a person who likes to grapple with issues and explore their theoretical underpinnings, I find it especially exciting that my ministry puts me in a position where so many intellectual currents converge.

Another reason that I find my ministry satisfying is that it allows me to use my talents for planning, organizing and problem solving in an environment which is value-based. Even though I regularly do many tasks that I might also be performing if I were working for another non-profit institution or in government the awareness that I am operating within and for a faith community produces a meaning all its own. Perhaps it is the consciousness that our efforts are directed toward spiritual goals, or the altruism and the dedication of my colleagues, or simply the bond of faith we all share that best explains why the climate is unique. In any case, I feel particularly fortunate to be doing what I have gifts for in a setting which enables me to recognize them as gifts connected with a call to ministry.

Being a manager for the institutional Church is not necessarily a new phenomenon. Bishops and deacons held such responsibilities from the earliest days of the Church. More recently, priests customarily held most of the administrative positions on a diocesan staff. Nowadays, at least in our diocese, the balance is shifting. At the present time, three of our five diocesan positions in educational administration are held by laymen. When I joined the diocesan staff eight years ago, all the administrator roles were filled by priests. Thus, I feel a bit like a pioneer. I sense that I and my colleagues are cutting a new path for the shared ministry of laity and clergy as the Church continues its pilgrimage. This is a satisfying and particularly humbling experience.

It is a daily struggle for me to keep my managerial style and practices ministerial rather than corporate in the secular sense. Because a large diocese like mine tends to look and operate like a corporation, it is easy to adopt a strictly corporate attitude toward diocesan staff work. For example, there is a temptation to adopt standard operating procedures or to hide behind policy positions as an excuse for not encountering people individually and ministering to them in unique situations. Fortunately, I find that such a temptation often is banished by the diversity and novelty of the issues which flow through my office. Many of the issues have not been around long enough to have prompted any routine way of dealing with them.

Another circumstance which keeps me aware of molding my management style into a ministry is the diversity of my staff. The staff is composed of priests, a deacon, a nun, two married couples, and several single and married laypersons. Of necessity, then, I must relate to each in different ways. Their situations in life are different. They have varying degrees of formal commitment to ministry. The Church has bound itself to different obligations regarding each of them. For reasons like these I feel that I exercise a dimension of my ministry when I reach out to each, challenging them and holding them accountable according to their circumstances, their obligations and their gifts.

As much as I try to touch the lives of my staff members in healing, challenging and enabling ways, I'm even more conscious of trying to bring to my Church management role a perspective which is distinctively lay. As long as diocesan staffs were composed mostly of clergy and religious it seemed congruent that the management bias would flow from a clerical worldview. Now that the staffing patterns are changing, it seems right to introduce another perspective. This means facing such issues as meaningful lay participation in decision making, realistic role expectations, accountability and performance evaluation, just and flexible compensation arrangements, providing a measure of job security and mobility within the system, etc. In this regard I face the temptation of making the lay perspective adversarial to rather than complementary to the clerical worldview. It will take time and patience for me and my colleagues to learn how to accept legitimate diversity and to minister in mutuality.

Sharing these reflections about my life and career as a lay minister would be incomplete if I did not say something about frustration. My principal frustration is connected with time, availability and expectations. In more abstract terms, this probably would be termed a difficulty with role identity. Because my ministry is a career based on a call and fundamental stance toward life, it is easy to say that I'm always ministering. But I can't always be working, even though there always seem to be enough tasks to fill an eighty hour week. Knowing when and how to draw the line between professional life and private life when a consciousness of being minister pervades both is not easy.

Many career lay ministers, including myself, received some formation in seminaries and religious communities. The ideals instilled in those years included being always available for service and attempting to meet all expectations. I still carry around those ideals but find, much to my frustration, that they cannot be realized as completely in a lay minister's life. Perhaps they never could be in the life of a priest or religious either. Nonetheless, whether they are adequate or not, role models do exist for ordained ministers. I haven't found the same thing yet for lay ministers, especially for those who are making a career of their calling. But we are in the early laps of the race. In fact, we've just barely begun to run. I have a firm hope that, if I and all my brother and sister lay ministers can glimpse and hold fast to a vision, we can keep running without tiring.

Edwina Gately

A Missionary Dream

I was mesmerized. Sitting on one of the back pews in the cathedral church of my home town in Lancashire, England, I listened spellbound to the missionary priest standing in the pulpit, telling exciting stories of an exotic continent called Africa. I heard about thick jungles, villages of poor, hungry black children, tropical fruits, wild animals, and grass huts. It was romantic, compelling, and from that moment on my decision was made—I was going to be a missionary. I could hardly wait to get through school so that I could fly off to the African bush and start converting.

It was the mid-1960's, and, naturally, the only way to be a missionary was to be a religious or a priest. So dutifully, and with great zeal, I attached myself to a missionary congregation and flew off to Africa in 1964. I was twenty-one, enthusiastic, an extrovert, and very naive. My missionary vision extended not much further than my nose and notions about black babies, illiteracy, and the urgency of salvation. My vision of missionary activity was all the missionary congregations running lots of hospitals, schools, and seminaries, and building bigger and better churches for the people. My vision of my own calling was that I would make it to be a *real* missionary when I made it to be a sister.

By the end of my first year of teaching in a mission school in Africa, most of my comfortable illusions had fled. The most devastating horror was the gradual realization that I did not have a religious vocation. This closed for me the only door that existed for a missionary activity and life commitment to mission. I experienced panic, disbelief, and a profound disappointment in God who cheated me out of a vocation. The sisters then advised me to wait and to reapply a year or two later. Determined to prove that I could "make the grade" (both to God and to the sisters) I went off to live in an African bush village to become the "ideal missionary."

Those two years in the village, running a small bush school and sharing the lifestyle of the people, served as the most important formation for my life commitment to lay ministry. My notions of mission were turned upside down. Suddenly I was the child, not the teacher. I could not speak the language. I did not know how to cook the traditional food. I was unfamiliar with customs and taboos. I remember one occasion when a visiting missionary brought me a zebra leg as a gift. In great joy I took it to a local African family so that we could all share the treat. They were aghast and deeply disturbed. They refused my generous gift. It was months later that I learned that their tribal symbol (and therefore taboo) was the zebra. My "gift" in their culture was an insult.

Although the people were materially poor and physically undernourished, I soon discovered that I needed them more than they needed me. As they began to teach me their language and their ways, I found in them an openness and a humility that moved me deeply. They received me, white and foreign, as a member of their own family and tribe, and I began to realize that their experience of God and faith was deeply embedded in their roots and their culture. I discovered that they saw God everywhere—in the trees, the earth, the plants, the seasons. These "pagans" were soaked in God. I began to wonder who was the missionary and the minister.

I remember one day when there was a lot of political unrest in the country, and it was almost impossible to get supplies. We were all hungry. As I was sitting outside my mud house, a little old lady, almost bent double, hobbled toward me from the forest. In her hands she clutched a small parcel wrapped in banana leaves. She thrust the parcel into my hands and said, "Thank you for staying with us." Then she hobbled back into the forest to her ramshackle straw hut. Inside the banana leaves lay three tiny chicken eggs—representing a small fortune at that time. I thought of the widow's mite. The old lady had given everything to me. I felt humbled down to my toes. I was learning to receive, and to listen to the God *already there*.

Just as my notions of mission were being turned upside down, so, too, were my notions of ministry. As I got to know the people more and learned their language, I began to realize that they accepted and valued me *as I was*—a Christian, a friend. I knew that I was ministering and being ministered to—but without the labels. I also saw that there was a great need for Christians with teaching and nursing skills to come and share their talents and their friendship with the African peoples. I saw that there was a real need for lay missionaries. But perhaps more important was a growing belief that we, as Westerners, in our self-confidence, our arrogance and stances of power, needed to learn from the people of the third world. I began to believe that we would not grow as a Church unless we were exposed and vulnerable enough to allow "the poor" to show us our poverty.

All these new thoughts, challenges, and questions left me confused and rather afraid. I felt very small before a great ecclesial institution that was convinced it had its act together and its vocations in nice neat little boxes. Much of the time I was afraid to deal with the questions and doubts about mission and ministry that kept coming into my mind. Then, in 1967, I became very ill with chronic malaria and a few other things, and

I reluctantly returned to my home country, England. It was a terrible wrench and a very lonely time. It was the beginning of a very painful and dark "Part II" of my formation for ministry.

I still wanted to be a missionary, though I had now accepted the fact that it was not to be as a member of a religious order. But I knew that, for all its joys and learning, living as the only European in an African village was fraught with loneliness and problems. Lack of support and affirmation was a major difficulty, as was the very real experience of not being a recognized part of the Church's missionary effort. No one at home understood what was happening to me. They thought that three years in Africa should have got "this missionary thing" out of my system. The apparent hopelessness of the situation combined with family and social pressures to "settle down and forget the whole thing" persuaded me that there was, in fact, no alternative but to do just that.

So, gritting my teeth in a mighty effort to forget my dream of being a missionary, I found myself a teaching job, an apartment, and a boy friend.

The year (1968) dragged by. I was restless, sad, unfulfilled. Deep down I was in despair. I could not forget Africa and the people I loved there; I could not forget the joy and enthusiasm which the thought of mission filled me with; I could not, in effect, deny my vocation to full-time ministry in the Church. I prayed, I cried, I yelled at God. I even went on retreat! (For lay people to do that in England is quite a drastic action!)

Then one day I happened to come across the Vatican Council documents. I read those dealing with "The Missionary Activity of the Church" and "The Apostolate of the Laity." What I read had a powerful effect on me, and brought together in my mind a new and exciting way for all people to be fully involved in missionary activity. The Vatican Council documents stated the importance of all Christians fulfilling

their baptismal call to mission, of being given proper formation and support, and of gathering together in international
groups for planning and organization.

I was encouraged and excited. Affirmation! *And* from the
Vatican!

I wrote a paper on the need to start a lay missionary movement, and how such a movement would function. My own experiences and lack of preparation for Africa led me to put
formation as a vital part of missionary activity. *Support*, both
overseas and after returning, was also important, as were *community* and a real *sense of belonging. Lay leadership* was, of course,
necessary for a lay movement. Then, believing that my commitment to this dream had to be all or nothing, I gave up my
hard won job and cherished apartment (and boy friend), and
began traveling around the country explaining my vision to
anyone who would listen—sisters, laypeople, priests, and
bishops. I gave talks, addressed various small groups, and
wrote articles for publication. I was burning with the conviction that not only were the laity called to mission, but that the
Church should facilitate and support this new and fragile
dream. It was a hard time because as I was not earning a salary, I had to live on charity, accepting whatever money, food,
or hospitality was offered. I have clear memories of being
handed a bag of oranges, a couple of sandwiches, and five dollars for my bus fare to the next town. The hardest thing was
the disbelief I encountered. Perhaps, looking back, it is under-
standable. I was young and not schooled in Church diplo-
macy. The sight of this mini-skirted, made-up young woman
smoking a cigarette and talking about lay missionaries must
have baffled some of the elderly monsignors and bishops on
whose doors I knocked. The vision I saw so clearly was too un-
real for some and too frightening for others.

My efforts, my enthusiasm, and my passionate conviction
seemed all to no avail. Why should they believe in me? Why

invest money or property in me? By the end of 1968 I was dispirited and weary and ready to give up the whole dream. But then I had a brainwave. I still had a hope left—John Cardinal Heenan, the archbishop of Westminster. An interview with the cardinal was my last attempt to win support for the foundation of a lay missionary movement.

I remember how nervous I was when the great moment for my meeting with the great man arrived. We met in a splendid parlor surrounded by massive oil paintings of past "princes of the Church." I was terrified. Would the cardinal say yes to lay missionaries? I was not prepared for the kind of questions he asked me: "Are you trying to start a religious order?" "A secular institute?" "Will you take vows or promises?" I did not want any of these things. I only wanted to share with him my vision of a lay missionary movement, autonomous and free and led by laypeople. The cardinal was clearly not impressed by my rather vague but urgent dream. At the end of the interview, he declared that the Church was not ready for the kind of lay missionary movement that I envisaged. He considered that the time was premature.

Once again I was totally disillusioned by the Church as I experienced it. To be lay and to be missionary was, it seemed, to be alienated and "on your own." If that was the only way to be a lay missionary, so be it. A few weeks after my interview with the cardinal, I returned to Africa, all set to carry on alone. I had had enough of a Church that could not even acknowledge the existence of laity in mission.

Since then I have learned how powerfully God works when we remove ourselves from the scene of the action and give the Holy Spirit enough space to give birth to a new creation. In my absence a number of missionary superiors got together and talked about the dream I had shared. They decided that it should, after all, be supported, and they wrote to me offering a house and a starting grant. In January 1969 I returned to England at their invitation, and in April of that year the missionary movement (known as the Volunteer Missionary Movement) began in London. The VMM came to birth through a great deal of pain, bewilderment, and chaos. But then most births involve those kinds of things. What is important is that we be open to the new things happening in the Church, and that we prepare with joy to see what God will reveal to us through his new works.

The VMM has, since its foundation, sent hundreds of men and women to serve as lay missionaries in twenty-six countries throughout the world. We have discovered together that new wine must be poured into new wineskins. We are struggling to discover our spirituality and charism in a Church which, up until recently, hardly acknowledged our existence; we are struggling with questions of community and authority, formation, and mission at home, as well as in the third world. They are not easy questions, but we are new and young and must make many mistakes. We are also confident, knowing that our mission comes from the Spirit who is ever creating new and strange things in our pilgrim Church.

Much of what is new we hope to bring back to our home church from the third world church. We share with our families and communities at home the gifts and the joys we have experienced in living with the people of the poor world; we share their faith, their hopes, and their enthusiasm. We share their vision of God so that we might become more aware that all are called and all are invited to the table. We hope that one day we will take away all the labels and there will be no reservations at the table—only a great celebration for all.

Carole Eipers

"My Ticket to the Kingdom"

I envision my story of lay ministry being depicted by a two-panel cartoon. In panel one, labeled "Yesterday," I am at a cocktail party surrounded by "everymans" who ask, "Do you work or do you teach?"

In panel two, labeled "Today," I am sitting alone at a desk which really isn't mine doing lesson plans for my junior high religion classes. A sheet of looseleaf taped to the front of the desk reads, "LAY MINISTER."

Below the two panels is the familiar caption, "You've come a long way, baby!"

I guess I have, though the change has been less in what I do than in how others perceive what I do. Recognition is important. Religion texts today define ministry as that which is "recognized by the community." It's nice, but for me not necessary. Whether people regard my teaching as equal to being unemployed, or they see it as lay ministry, as long as I am called to teach, I will teach.

Some definitions of ministry are exclusive—"clergy only"; some are so watered down they are meaningless. Some equate ministry with celibate lifestyle and seem to imply that marriage and ministry are mutually exclusive. Even the term "lay" ministry implies a "second best" which sees ministry as competition with other Christians rather than commitment to Christ.

My personal definition of ministry is the expression of my vocation in service to others. My vocation is to be a Christian. I fulfill that vocation in my roles as wife, mother, teacher, parishioner, and writer through service to my family, my parish and the larger community.

Ministry is neither simply what I do, nor just what I am; ministry is what I do with what I am. More precisely, ministry is what I am called to be and to do with my particular gifts and limitations.

There are those who ask, "Can anything a thirty-eight year old woman does properly be called ministry?" I have asked myself in the midst of a parish spaghetti dinner, "Can a thirty-eight year old woman minister in overalls and a moustache?"

I am not certain how others would answer those questions, but I have answered them for myself. Yes, I, lay woman, with or without my moustache glued on, am ministering when my teaching or my clowning proceeds as my response to a loving Father and out of love for my brothers and sisters. My ministry is affirmed when my fellow parishioners laugh, and when my students learn.

My primary ministry is teaching junior high religion in our parish school. Together we share the content and experiences of our Church's faith and our personal faith.

My secondary ministries include working with our C.C.D. teachers, writing for religious education and ministry publications, giving workshops, lectures and retreats for other parishes, and developing audio-visual presentations for meetings and parish celebrations.

I see teaching as my primary ministry not only in terms of time and energy spent, but also because it is in this context that I am able most fully and appropriately to share and grow in my own faith and invite others to do so as well. Religion is not a "subject-to-be-taught" but a relationship between God and his people to be formed and strengthened. I see my task as helping my students to discern the on-going revelation of a loving Father in our lives and inviting their response. I try to do this as Jesus did: not by preaching the good news but by trying to *be* the good news of love, acceptance, forgiveness, and resurrection. Therefore, my relationship with my students takes precedence over grades, discipline, and other academic facets. My ministry calls me first to love my students, to listen to them, and, when there is an opportunity to serve others, to say, "We'll do it together," for it is in those moments of working together that we form a community.

One of the major turning points in my ministry occurred seven years ago when my family had returned to live in my childhood parish and I began to teach in our school. I taught reading and one religion class, and found that the religion class was the one which both consumed my energy and re-energized me as well. Over the next four years I felt myself drawn by my own background and gifts to teach religion full-time. This inner calling was reinforced by student evaluations and the less formal "I hope I get you for religion" remarks. Parents affirmed my call by requesting me as their child's religion teacher. Eventually a change in faculty brought about an invitation from the administration, and with the blessing of colleagues I took on the entire junior high religion program. I began to expand the core experiences of spiritual journal writing, service and liturgical celebration, and to see the possibilities for growth in faith over a two-year period. It has been exciting and exhausting.

Now not only I, but my students as well, are called to minister. Their gifts are recognized and affirmed by our parish and our community. We can share our experiences of what it means to minister: the rewards, the disappointments, the difficulties and the satisfactions. Whether we are cleaning the parish grounds, spending time with disabled children, or dramatizing a parish reconciliation celebration, my students develop an awareness of the possibilities for ministry and build up a repertoire of positive responses to the needs they see around them. They learn, through serving with and for this Christian community, that they are needed and capable, that they belong.

I cannot give what I do not have; I cannot ask of my students what I am not willing to do myself. Along with them I keep a journal, I continue to learn about our faith, I pray, I reflect on my life in the light of the Gospel, I serve, and I struggle to live what I believe and teach.

My students are my greatest challenge to growth and my most constant means of support. Their openness and honesty, their examples of unconditional love and generosity call me to be more than I am. When we first went to the Misericordia Homes for Disabled Children, it was my students who reached out to hold those children first; it was they who more readily saw beyond the wheelchairs and braces to the persons. It was their expectations of me that gave me the strength to reach out and see beyond as well.

As much as they challenge me, these students support my efforts in a way that perhaps the adult community no longer can. The students are willing to take the Gospel seriously; they do not need to water it down nor mold it to fit their lives nor justify their decisions. They lack the cynicism of adults; they are open to their tradition and to changes which the Spirit may ask of them and of our Church. It has been my students who have salvaged my idealism when it has run aground or has been smashed on the rocks of reality. They have needed me and affirmed me when I felt unneeded and unaffirmed by the adult community. They have recognized my need for encouragement and have accepted not only my gifts, but my limitations. My students have in so many ways gifted me in the very ways I hope to gift them.

My secondary ministries flow from my teaching. I serve at many parish functions, not as example for my students, but rather as invitation.

Ministry to students leads to involvement with their parents and families. I am sometimes a bridge between generations, called to help each understand the other. I find myself attempting to heal student hurts caused by families, or vice versa. I encourage, through student notes and gifts, a growth in appreciation for their families, and by frequent communication with parents I try to foster their appreciation for the goodness and giftedness of their children.

I have worked with our C.C.D. teachers developing processes for use with their students, first on an informal "Can I ask you about this?" basis, and now in a more formal capacity as one of their "master teachers."

Another outgrowth of my primary ministry has been the opportunity to write for religious education journals and ministry publications. This is a double blessing, for it not only allows me to share the successful experiences of my classroom ministry and my personal reflections on the Gospel, but it has provided an outlet for my creativity which must be superseded by my students' creativity in our classes.

There are other secondary ministries which I find rewarding and challenging, other involvements I seek because I also need to express my faith on an adult level. I began a Master of Pastoral Studies program and received my degree; I am working in our parish RENEW program; I make retreats, and my husband conducts a Scripture study group for my junior high colleagues and me.

I am not the Messiah; I know I cannot be all things to all people; I simply want to be all I can for those I am with at any given moment. This means that each year I must reluctantly let go of graduates, of parents who have become friends, to concentrate my energies on the new faces which approach. It means sometimes turning from the ninety-nine to seek the one whose need is greatest. It means being humble enough to turn to others who can serve a particular need better than I. It means having faith in the one real Messiah and his ability to work miracles—to turn even our most watery efforts into fine wine.

That piece of looseleaf taped to my desk reads "LAY MINISTER," and it is a precious title, but not a mixed blessing. The cost has been dear, and those who love me must share the price.

My husband and our son have paid for my ministry with time we could have spent together. They, and I, have paid financially, both in outlay for my courses and in income which could be ours if I were to ply my trades in a secular field. They have paid by eating fast-food meals when I am busy (though I must add my son considers this a definite benefit) and they have paid by sharing not only the housework, but the hurts and frustrations of my work.

There has been a price for those who call me friend. I am not always available to them, and often they are "dragged in" to an event or a celebration out of loyalty to me. I know they are hurt when others criticize me, frustrated because, while they have accepted my work, they sometimes have not really understood. They have recognized that part of me will always be intensely lonely, and that they can never fill that loneliness which is assuaged only by a vision of the Kingdom. Sometimes they are left helpless at the sight of my tears.

I too have paid a price for my ministry. There are some whose friendship itself I have been asked to pay because they could not understand that involvement in the Church is not optional for me. I have given up titles, power, and wealth which perhaps I could have acquired in another field. I have paid my leisure time so that I might be available to those I serve yet still get dinner ready, do the laundry, and be at my son's soccer game.

I have paid the price of sometimes feeling that my worth depends on what I do rather than who I am. I have paid the price of fear for my future in a field where there is little upward mobility for a woman whose family might one day be dependent on her income.

I have—and am—paying the price of the loneliness of the lay minister. I am not clergy, I am not a religious, yet because of my background, education, and commitment, many fellow laity see me as "not quite one of them." It is lonely to be with those who "do what I do" but do not perceive it as ministry and therefore do not feel the need to form community as I do. There has been the loneliness of seeing effective laypeople leave their ministries for better paying positions, not because of greed, but for survival. There has been a painful lack of support and the realization that if one is competent it is assumed that he or she needs no thanks or encouragement. There has been the idea that a good lay minister must know when things go right, and so only needs to be told about his or her errors. Perhaps the greatest price of all is learning to love and let go, to call students not to myself but to the Lord. There is an incomparable joy in seeing them go to him, and an unutterable loneliness as well.

If my faith has grown deeper, my doubts spring from new depths too. I have times of utter hopelessness in my faith when all the words ring empty and all the symbols seem hollow. At those moments I rediscover the meaning of laying down my life.

As my eighth graders celebrated confirmation this year, I cried. I cried for all I could not or would not be for them. I cried for what our Church fails to say and to be. I cried for the moments of doubt they face in their futures, and I even wondered if perhaps I had lied to them. Yet, as they committed themselves, I recommitted myself and I realized how much their faith strengthens mine and how much their belief helps me to believe, even when the message of Jesus does not seem to "work" for me. I realized, too, in the midst of my tears, that compassion can be purchased only through suffering, and I was glad to have cried.

I see my call to ministry as gift; I see my gifts as my call to ministry. All of my adult life I have pursued the Lord—or he has pursued me. I spent seven years in religious life, two years as a single woman in ministry, and the past eleven as wife and mother in ministry. Though my path has changed, the destination has remained consistent. Always I have chosen in response to Jesus' "Come, follow me" as I hear it, as he speaks to me in prayer, the Scriptures, the wisdom of our community and its tradition, and through my friends.

St. Paul said, "The manifestation of the Spirit is given to each person for the common good." His words have become a keynote in my teaching, and I have come to treasure my own gifts in proportion to their usefulness to those I serve.

The rewards of my ministry are a hundredfold: a hug, a smile, a student's act of faith. There is the joy of seeing them possess the knowledge to ask the questions which they need answered, the joy of seeing them have the strength to live with unanswered and even unanswerable questions. I know the joy of sharing their idealism, their enthusiasm to serve, their daring to reach out, their spontaneous laughter and love. I am repaid when I see them grow in compassion, in an awareness of the needs around them; I find joy as they discover possibilities which I never saw. I am rewarded by the joy of knowing that they realize their own goodness and giftedness.

Six of my eighth grade girls stayed overnight with me recently. We ate pizza, told stories, and laughed, and they informed me that they had signed us up to pray at midnight for our parish prayer vigil. As we sat on the floor in our den praying by candlelight, I knew the incredible joy of realizing that in many ways they had grown beyond me. They had surpassed me in their ability to pray, to be honest with themselves and with each other, to articulate their faith and their struggles. I saw how much more readily they are able to separate the accidentals from the essential of simple faith in Jesus. I felt tremendous joy in knowing that the message of Jesus is in their hands and the vision of the Kingdom is in their hearts. On that evening I felt my ministry affirmed by the Spirit himself, and as I basked in that affirmation, I think I heard that Spirit laugh and say, "You mean *our* ministry, don't you?"

If I have found great joy on the heights, I have grown to know the paradoxical joy of finding Jesus in the depths. As I have grown in faith, I have discovered that Jesus is no longer a "good luck charm" which brings only success and support, health, love and rewards. He is a constant companion in crucifixions and resurrections, the One who is willing to support me when others fail, the One who touches that intensely lonely core of my being with his vision of the Father's Kingdom when my sight is blurred by disappointment.

I have known the unsurpassable joy of momentary glimpses of that Kingdom: when someone trusts, when someone forgives, when someone finally gives that long-withheld hug, when someone believes in love enough to risk giving of self, when there is laughter in the midst of tragedy because we suffer together. I have glimpsed the Kingdom as I sit before the Lord opening my heart, unashamed of my mistakes and willingly weary. I have seen the Kingdom in the support of my family, friends and students.

My dream is that our community will become that Kingdom of God. The reality, to paraphrase the caption on my two-panel cartoon, reads, "You've got a long way to go, baby!" The question for me is not one of searching elsewhere for the dream, but, rather, of reaching our dream of the Kingdom with this, the reality of our parish.

I strive to proclaim the Gospel faithfully, not only knowing but willingly admitting how far I fall short of what Jesus asks. I let my students know that faith is a gift and a challenge, and I do not pretend to be without the struggle to believe and to live that belief. I try to struggle always with an alleluia—sometimes on my lips, occasionally caught in my throat. I try not to hide my own fears, frustrations, doubts and tears, but to say, yes, in spite of all this, the Kingdom is worth it.

Who knows—perhaps one day an old dog-eared sheet of looseleaf that says "LAY MINISTER" may just be my ticket to that Kingdom.

David A. Ramey

A Different Gift

That is why I kneel before the Father from whom every family in heaven and on earth takes its name; and I pray that he will bestow on you gifts in keeping with the riches of his glory. May he strengthen you inwardly through the working of his Spirit. May Christ dwell in your hearts through faith, and may charity be the root and foundation of your life. Thus you will be able to grasp fully, with all the holy ones, the breadth and length and height and depth of Christ's love, and experience this love which surpasses all knowledge, so that you may attain to the fullness of God himself. To him whose power now at work in us can do immeasurably more than we ask or imagine—to him be glory in the church and in Christ Jesus through all generations, world without end. Amen (Eph 3:14–21).

In accepting the invitation to take part in this project of offering some insights into "the real stories of those who are in lay ministry," I find it important to remind myself that the "real" story is an ancient one, best captured for me in the prayer uttered by Paul to his friends long ago. While the story is dated in origin it is vibrant and vital in the lives of those who attempt to keep it alive today through their work and service.

To this end, of offering a current interpretation with some vitality and hope to a timeless and no less vibrant reality,

I offer a few shades of my own experience of a career commitment to a ministry of all believers.

CHANGING MOTIVATIONS

"That is why I kneel before the Father . . . ." The image or position that most represents my own experience of a ministry of all believers or "lay ministry" is that of kneeling before our Creator. After more than ten years of full-time service in some ministerial setting, I find myself, in more pensive moments, asking the perennial question: "Why am I doing this?"

Ten years later I find my answers coming more in terms of contemplating my life orientations and reflection on personal motivations rather than in the articulation of a clear rationale. The image of kneeling before the Father is one that intrigues me when I consider the many motivations I have operated from in my career of service.

ECCLESIASTICAL AND PERSONAL RECOGNITION

In my earliest years, fresh from a theological school, exegesis in hand and little else, I recall my first orientation toward lay ministry to be more focused on a desire for some basis of ecclesiastical recognition to provide a sense of personal esteem. Appropriately my wife and I accepted positions as liturgists for a campus ministry setting in a large urban Catholic university. As one may expect, the choice of a university liturgical setting provided the occasion for much challenge, and disappointment for one concerned with being as important as one's clerical brothers. Without chronicling numerous experiences, liturgy was (and may still be) a symbolic stillpoint for demonstrating public recognition in an ecclesiastical world, where recognition is ritualized and formalized in every movement and mode of dress and behavior. While hopefully making some positive contributions to this community's understanding of liturgical practice, I also learned that in a ministerial world which has a recognized and defined system of representing religious authority, the real roots of religious authority emerge less from formal, sanctioned, or liturgical symbols, and more from the substance and foundations of one's own life of service to others.

COMMUNAL AND ECCLESIAL SERVICE

Beyond my early adulthood struggles for identity that were heightened by a unique ministerial choice in my earlier years, I moved not only in location but in spirit and motivation to a different place in my search for a continued lay ministry. I was blessed to accept a diocesan office position for a rural-urban diocese in the upper midwest. My particular role responsibilities were to facilitate the development of leadership and commitment to adult education among parishes of the diocese. There was a decidedly different "feel" from this work than I had experienced in my earlier career. As I hear others describe similar events, there was a distinctive pioneering and missionary dedication that I brought to this work and which I believe shaped the overwhelmingly positive responses that I recall and cherish. In retrospect, while I had certainly learned more skills, acquired a new degree, and interpersonally matured, the major difference was the motivation or intentionality toward ministry that I brought to its demands. Far less concerned with the needs for recognition and esteem by Church officials, I focused my attention on building in modest ways the communal and collective body of Church membership that

I was able to impact. Even if "Father knew best" his congregation and he had some things to learn about adults and adult life and how to nurture it effectively. My personal desires for esteem matured into a desire for greater competence. My increased competence produced greater effectiveness among those I served. My motivations became transformed into a commitment that others will recognize they have a valued contribution to make to the ecclesial reality we call "Church." For this middle period of lay ministry, satisfaction came from the enthusiasm others gained for their ability to learn and develop religious sensitivity. Assisting others on their journey to life-giving relationships in the local church replaced the need for official sanctions by others as a motivation for ministry. Similar to how I imagine Paul, the blessings of Jerusalem became much less important than the blessedness of those I worked with and for. I believe that in this transition I found a much appreciated deliverance from much of the frustration and sometimes bitterness or "burnout" I have encountered among some lay colleagues in ministry.

ECCLESIOLOGICAL SERVICE TO THE WORLD

After several satisfying years of service in a diocesan adult education role, in the words of a colleague I once again had "sand in my shoes." However, the sands of change became much heavier as I began to ask the long-term question: "Can anyone survive in lay ministry for life?" Three children later, my family and I once again found ourselves on a journey that demanded the changing and adapting of life's relationships, new work assignments, and yet another career path in ministry. The consequences and results of a changing career in ministry became more apparent, as did a new slant on my personal motivations.

I accepted the directorship of a large ministerial staff at a religious conference center. This enterprising and often tenuous balance of ministerial service with financial viability placed me in a career phase far from the immediate rewards and recognition of a university liturgical setting and distinct from the work of building parish leadership in an established and defined diocesan system. Our raising and responding to the meaning questions of life are contingent on audiences who pay for our ministerial service and whose participation relies on their experiencing greater satisfaction and enrichment from our programs than would disposing of their few discretionary dollars in other ways. Motivationally I had also shifted again. Personal and family security is ever present, and in this role I can attain some technological, business, and marketing skills should I need to pursue an alternate career later in life. But more profoundly I came to believe that a career commitment to lay ministry is a commitment to the development of human community beyond parochial and established parish settings. The spirits of resourcefulness and creativity that are demanded of our work as a conference center not only involve our survival but reflect our commitment and my personal motivation. The meaning of a Church's ministry is in responding to a call of a wider world in need of development and enrichment. The ecclesiastical and ecclesiological motivations of serving in the Church and for the Church are limited for me. My own understanding of why one may choose a lay ministry career have shifted to include a mission to a world of market places in need of some "good news." My current questions about lay ministry focus more on its symbolic power to serve as a reminder to others that they can and do make a difference by their part in the human community. This has challenged me to a vision and intentionality of lay ministry as a service to the world, through the Church perhaps, but not only in and for the Church.

INNER STRENGTHS

"May he strengthen you inwardly through the workings
of his Spirit . . . ." Among many colleagues and acquaintances
I have encountered pursuing careers in lay ministries, I consider myself most fortunate. In all of my positions I have had
and continue to enjoy trusted and trusting peer relationships.
I find myself in a somewhat ironic situation of supervising a
large staff of primarily religious women, men and clergy. The
customary struggles or tensions of lay-clergy, male-female,
and power and authority relationships have been a part of my
experience. But they have not overshadowed it. Often it is
easy to attribute my fortunate path to "luck" or "grace" or
skill. While all of these have played their part, I suppose, a primary resource I have found in others and myself who have
become "survivors" in ministry careers is a unique inner
strength.

Lay ministries in the Church today are filled with many
tensions and struggles. From a continued education in management training and consulting I believe that these struggles also exist in any mobile career path. Power, control,
recognition, and esteem are all factors in most developing career experiences. What I find different about these issues in
the ministerial context is that ministers desire to either tran-
scend these needs or avoid them. We don't expect to have them
in the Church. Our perceptions of these issues and their importance is what may heighten the expectations we have for
our success in lay ministry. For example, if we believe that
clergy and laity should work together cooperatively in colleague roles to serve others, when we encounter the "power of
the cloth" executed upon us inappropriately, we are bound for
disappointment.

A perceptual lens that I have endeavored to bring to these
situations during my career is a simple psychological princi-

ple, "Explore the devil within." To the extent that the indiscretions of others in ministry have made my career pursuits problematic, I have found a lingering issue within that has given these situations that power over me. Perhaps my own saving grace in pursuing a career ministry as a layperson has been my sometimes reluctant but persistent desire to explore what in myself has given "clericalism," for example, so much energy over my response to it. My most frequent prayer in ministry continues to be: "What in this am I called to learn?" What I have gained from my periodic struggles is a real inner strength. The longer my career extends, and the more I mature, the less I feel controlled by the occasional condescending attitudes of my clerical brothers and my sisters and brothers in religious life. The more I have also become able to face the experience of having my thoughts dismissed by fellow laity because they come from "someone just like them."

This pursuit of inner strength has spawned a deep-seated and continuous quest within myself to become more competent and adept in what I can offer, and to believe in my own competence to the extent that it is real and used to promote appropriate ends. I believe that too many of us in lay ministry secretly long for the instant credibility that we perceive clergy and religious to have. When it is not given over to us, we feel treated like poor handmaidens. In fact we may be called to experience precisely what the Gospel expects in our time—to exemplify effective, realistic, and articulate ways to share the real complexity of the "good news" in ways people will apply it and live it in their lives. I have learned to view the instant recognition and deference given to other ministerial lifestyles as a way for those who offer it to put the challenge of spirituality at arm's length in their own lives, as if holiness were reserved for others. For those receiving it, deference and shallow recognition is one more burden to overcome in assessing their own genuine inner strengths.

PERENNIAL STRUGGLES

"May Christ dwell in your hearts through faith, and may charity be the root and foundation of your life." Despite an overriding experience of success and enjoyment in a career ministry, these last ten years have also been etched with recurring and perennial struggles. The editors have asked me in this series that we be candid about what others may expect. The issues of stable personal lifestyle, monetary success, and ultimate security continue to surface in lay career ministries, often in increasingly complex forms. Pious as it may seem, at times the only response I am able to assemble is a prayer for faith and charity.

In the early years of a ministerial career I found myself advocating just salaries and compensation for laity in ministry. For others and myself this has been a symbolic and very practical way of claiming a rightful place in ministry. While I believe now that I basically enjoy a fair compensation, unlike many of my colleagues, an underlying concern over stability and permanence still exists. It has been my experience often in my career that I have asked my family also to share in a lifestyle of less than others of our talent and experience can enjoy. Those choices between a new wardrobe for a child and major dental work for myself or my spouse precipitate a certain guilt over whether it is ultimately fair to ask other loved ones to participate in a less than financially rewarding enterprise. On the other hand I have convictions that a certain attitude of simplicity and vulnerability is important to Christian living. For me it is fine; for my children I still wonder if I can ask them for something they cannot comprehend or assent to. What also compounds the experience of this financial marginality is that those usually comforting colleagues in religious life and priesthood have basic life securities provided for. Their poverty is a more personal daily sacrifice rather than a systemic vulnerability. While they are models and examples for me in other ministerial concerns, here other models are scarce. This vulnerability became more acute in my life recently when a lay colleague in ministry died. Although the situation was adequately provided for due to a prior career in business, it gave me the occasion to think of the consequences of my own death for my family at this time.

Beyond simple financial considerations there is a deep-seated void of the traditional institutional support of people in ministry that is afforded to many Protestant clergy, our own clergy, and those in religious life.

Should the tragic or unexpected befall them there are some institutional safeguards to protect the vulnerability that their day-to-day sacrifice of personal resources occasions. For many in lay ministry there are varying degrees of day-to-day financial sacrifice, but for few if any are there any long-term safeguards against the unplanned for.

Another perennial tension that I and others in lay career ministries face is a certain discrepancy among standards of competence. One does not have to work long in a ministerial setting to witness less educated, less polished, less trained members of clergy or religious life receive positions or advancements that we might enjoy or perform more effectively. There is a certain corporate preference among equals and not so equals that I believe we will have to contend with for decades to come. As the shortage of clergy and religious ministers becomes more acute, the institutions they own and control will promote and locate them in prominent roles—sometimes despite their own desires and suitability. Perhaps this is appropriate; I'm not sure. I'm far less inclined to raise the standard-bearing language of injustice than I may have been a decade ago. For me, it is a corporate and institutional reality we endure, perhaps very similar to experiences in the business and industrial sector of our culture. Perhaps it is our own expectations through the ideals of ministry that may need to be modified to the realization that the Kingdom is not yet and will not be in the near future.

Throughout whichever perennial struggles we may have to address in career ministries, there have been resources for me to face the occasional marginality I experience.

The wisdom of faith sometimes invites and challenges me to live more easily with the unknown and unpredictable. The wonderings about tomorrow or even ten years from now would not add to the possibilities of today. Again the faith that sometimes emerges from the experiences of marginality in lay ministry may be a model of the kind of faith our culture is most desirous of possessing. Perhaps it is indeed a different security we possess and can share.

Charity and generosity have also been important correctives in my life through those experiences of marginality. For example, it has been more productive for me to take an educative and informative posture rather than a vindictive one toward those who may not understand or identify with the intensity or import of these issues. At the root of all human experiences is a certain living on the edge of existence. I have found this consciousness heightened through a career of lay ministry and ultimately to be a greater resource than a burden.

TIMELESS VISIONS

"To him whose power at work in us can do immeasurably more than we ask or imagine . . . ." I began my reflections by noting my changing motivations over the years in a career of lay ministry. I alluded to the contribution of lay ministry perhaps being best perceived as a symbolic reminder that individuals in the human community can and do make a difference. It is a grandiose vision to believe, in times of complex world views and the dominance of political, social, economic and religious systems over life, that individuals can create change. Perhaps one individual does not, but individuals with a shared vision of hope in the name of the creative power of God can. To me, what is characteristically and qualitatively different about lay ministry is precisely its marginality, its less than official stature, its ordinariness. From this perspective I view my own and others' contribution to lay ministry as being a simple and profound statement to others that we are all called in the human community precisely from our own ordinary talents and experience to make a difference. The meaning of lay ministry for me finds root in our Vatican II document "Lumen Gentium." What we can strive to become as a Church and its members is a symbol to others in our neighborhoods, congregations, cities, and the world, and that our giftedness in all its limitations, when allied with the giftedness of others, is the creative wisdom of God. Our gift perhaps is to serve as an invitation and sometimes a challenge for others to "attain to the fullness of God himself." Perhaps then the call of a lay minister is to be a different gift. I prefer the psychological language of generativity to understand this gift. If our contributions of service to the Church and beyond have meaning, they are as reminders to others that our individual and collective "common sense" is a reflection of the wisdom of God's fullness. Perhaps even more profoundly our collective ordinary wisdom is precisely the gift of generative care that a cautious, suspicious, "eye for an eye" world is most desirous of. For me, what makes a qualitative difference in my own life as a lay minister, and in the lives of those whom I've come to admire, is the realization that our gift is given beyond our capacity to realize or comprehend its ultimate impact. In the psychological virtue of generativity it is given most grace-fully in the realization that we may not have the satisfaction of knowing the outcome beyond knowing we have given it well. I've often described lay ministry as a mirror which we offer each other. "What you see in me you can do also."

What I am describing are my perceptions of an emerging ecclesiology for lay ministers. It is not only an internal tool for the Church to serve its members. Its best resources may lie in our ability to mirror to others that they share in the creative wisdom of God, and that through that wisdom the human community can transform Church, society and world to achieve "immeasurably more than we ask or imagine."

Lay ministry in all of its complex balance of excitement, disappointment, marginality, and frailty is a way of being human and offering a different yet ordinary gift to others, so that they in turn may come to do the same. As a consequence we may ultimately join in the ancient prayer of Paul, the disciple and lay minister: "To him be glory in the church and in Christ Jesus through all generations, world without end. Amen."

Karen Clements Claydon

Clown Ministry

New Year's Eve day I was standing on the street corner in the older section of our town when an old man passed me. He crossed the street and continued to walk. I was surprised that he didn't seem to notice but I continued to stand there, dressed in my clown attire. He suddenly stopped, turned around and came back. As he approached me I noticed how dirty and torn he was, unshaven, with mismatched clothes not unsimilar to my own. He said: "I thought that something seemed different about you." Since my clown character doesn't talk, I responded with a bow, and he countered it. He said that he hadn't seen many smiling faces lately and he just wanted to stop and say hello. I pulled a feather from my pocket and tickled him, and then presented him with the feather. "Thanks, I could use some laughter." I gave him a handful of confetti which he threw all over us and said: "You remembered! It's New Year's Eve tonight. We should have a party." At that point I discovered a rubber chicken in my pocket and a green checkered tablecloth. We dined elegantly on that and plastic eggs. He offered me a cigarette which I politely pretended to smoke; then, as I played Auld Lang Syne on my trumpet kazoo, we danced. When the song was over we were both crying. We hugged each other. I still had not said anything. His words to me were: "I can't remember ever havin' a New Year's party before. No one's ever loved me for nothin'." We hugged again and he walked off.

Such scenes have become a regular and cherished part of my life since becoming a clown minister.

I never really made a conscious effort to be a lay minister. As a young adult, I found myself re-examining the Roman Catholic religion that my parents had chosen for me at birth and even exploring some Protestant churches. I soon knew that I wanted to belong to a faith community. Along with my husband Moe, I chose a small Catholic university parish. Belonging to a church meant more to me than just attending Mass on Sundays and dropping my children off for religious education. I wanted to get to know the other families. I wanted to take advantage of religious classes myself. I wanted to be a vital part of the church family. So it seemed natural to want to share what I could. I responded to the call for religious education teachers, lectors, lay ministers of Communion to the sick and elderly and to the board of Catholic Social Services because those were areas in which I felt comfortable. Besides the "formal" lay ministry jobs, there were less noticed areas of ministry that just seemed natural as part of a church family: meals taken to ill parishioners, drives for clothes for the poor, talking to lonely college students away from home, organizing picnics and parties for the parish, etc.

One summer a class in clowning was offered at our church. I took the class and fell in love with clowning. It is an art, and like any art it takes a lot of time and dedication. That summer I wondered how I could care for my family which included our nine year old son Andrew and our eleven year old daughter Sage and a rather peculiar dog when I felt this new desire to run off and join the circus. I was delighted when they asked me to join their troupe. I took the role of the carpet clown which required less training and left me more time for my family and other ministries. A carpet clown works the crowds, greets the people, and in this particular circus tries to sneak into the performance.

I soon learned that being a carpet clown requires its own kind of skill—the ability to "read" people and anticipate their reactions, to not offend, to bring out the shy but not to embarrass. I loved this type of clowning because, unlike the stage performer clowns who had everything under control, I never knew what would happen and I liked the risk. Since I know God to be a God of surprises and a God that works through people, I was always scared but excited to see who would come and what interaction we would have.

I was so excited about the reaction we had on other people that I wanted to take the show on the road to charity groups. I felt that this was a gift we all had to share. We performed for a group of adults who worked with physically handicapped who don't get out often, and I saw the effect that the show had on them, but, most of all, the effect that their joy had on us as performers, and I knew in my heart that the clowning skill that I was working on could be a powerful ministry.

The birth of our third child Tim put my clowning on the back burner for two years. Then, in the summer of 1981, I discovered and attended a week-long workshop on clown ministry in Berkeley, California. I learned there that clowns all over the United States, England and other countries were using the art of clown to minister to people. Suddenly, I knew that I needed to re-evaluate all of the ministries I was involved with, for I felt called in a special way to the ministry of the clown. With four others I clowned on the subways and streets of San Francisco and Berkeley. At times I was scared; an arrow through the head may be funny, but a knife—well? I discovered that I enjoyed clowning for the people on the street. Many are out of work and forced to be where they don't want to be. There aren't many opportunities to laugh and play. Basic survival is serious. I have had many beautiful experiences on the street with people. I have come upon situations where I should be fearful, but somehow my clown character is so open and vulnerable that she loses the fear I might normally feel.

Because the street isn't the only place where people need the healing power of play and laughter, I find that my clown is welcomed at many places. I have clowned at nursing homes and homes for the physically and developmentally disabled and other institutions in our community. I drop in at our local hospitals whenever I can. I stroll through the lobby. The pink ladies say: "Oh, how cute. You must be going to the children's ward. They will just love you." I smile, do something to make them laugh, then head for the elevator. Sometimes I never leave it. A clown doesn't have to be funny all the time. There is such a fine line between sorrow and joy. I remember a lady who got on the elevator one day. We were all alone. She had just come from the surgical floor and she looked very sad. I respected her sadness, so I stayed very still. She finally looked in my eyes. The clown mask often reflects the feelings of the person who looks into it. I put my hand out to her. She took it, then embraced me. When the elevator door opened, she said, "Thank you. My husband is very ill but now I feel that there is hope."

I actually seldom make it to the children's ward. Children get lots of attention when they are ill. I usually go up to the nurse's desk on the regular floors. I have a little card that says: "Anyone here need cheering up?" The usual response is "Yes! We do." So that's where I start. If a doctor walks up, I sometimes "help" the doctor with rounds. And then it begins. Relatives stop me in the hall: "Please, just come to see my sick brother." Well, I don't ignore the relatives either. It's good for a family who has been through days of stress and worry together to laugh together. When I go into a room, I never know what to expect. Sometimes we laugh together, sometimes we cry. Some people I can tell don't want me there at all and I respect that. But if the nurse says: "Don't go into Room 103; I've never met anyone so grumpy and miserable," you can bet that when the nurse isn't looking, that is where I end up. I've yet to be disappointed.

Apart from the street, the place I like to clown the most is the supermarket on Saturday morning. Speaking of miserable, grumpy people! You wouldn't believe all the wonderful things a clown can do with a rubber chicken at the meat counter. Tensions dissolve into laughter, especially if the customer is complaining to the butcher about the quality of the meat. The parent with the screaming child can be grateful too. One day, I had a child ask: "Mommy, will you buy the clown please?" Even waiting in long lines doesn't seem so bad when you are being entertained.

Perhaps some people wouldn't call what I do a ministry, but God is a God of joy and celebration and unexpected surprises and a God who delights in simple things and I believe, also, a God who laughs and wants his people to laugh. Our Lord also showed us the importance of touch. In our often impersonal society, so many people are starving of skin hunger. A clown, for some reason, is allowed to touch, and often through this physical contact very real healings take place.

Because a clown is very visible and can easily get people's attention, I can use my clown to point out social injustices such as world hunger through skits on streets corners or in front of churches.

Jesus spoke in the simplest terms and with words and actions that went directly to the heart. My clown can bring God's presence to people in the simplest of ways in order for people to understand. I may clown during a liturgy in order to do this—not as a disruption, but as an interruption to make people pay attention or see the Gospels in a new light. The clowning can be very brief and subtle; it can encompass the entire liturgy or just a part.

My clown character is simple, silent, light-hearted, curious, always anticipating surprise, delighting in the wonders of God's creation, transforming everyday ordinary things into the extraordinary. Feeling people's response to her brings me alive to Jesus' words that we must become like little children in order to enter the Kingdom of heaven. I have begun to give retreat days, explaining the fool, the clown, as a reminder to ourselves to laugh, to play, to celebrate life and to remember that God doesn't take us as seriously as we take ourselves. The clown reminds us of the masks we hide behind and of the necessity to die to ourselves, to strip away the masks and become the beautiful, simple creation that God intended us to be. During the retreat we use clowning, music, play, movement and meditation to learn to become more vulnerable, loving, light-hearted children of God.

The clown is so simple and yet "accomplishes" so much that I am beginning to see how the clown can become a symbol of a simple lifestyle. As the line in Bernstein's Mass says, "God loves simple things, for God is the simplest of all." Simplicity is something I yearn for and strive for in my own life.

I sometimes find the expectations that others have of me frustrating. I constantly get calls from people who are working for worthwhile charities who could use a clown to help them celebrate an event. It's hard to say "no," especially when they might not understand. But my ministry is not to large groups of people but to people one on one. This leads to another frustration—time. There are times I would like to pop into a hospital for 20-30 minutes on my way home from clowning somewhere else, but I've never been there for less than two hours. It can easily become more and I *want* to stay. I also want to come back and follow-up on the people I encounter.

One day I walked into the room of a middle-aged gentleman. He laughed. I pulled out my rubber chicken from his food tray. He joked about the food. I painted his nose red to match mine. I shook his hand, left him a feather to tickle himself while I was gone, and went to leave. It was a fairly typical visit. Then he said, "Please don't go. I haven't laughed in such a long time." I noticed the tears coming, so I knew the time for laughter had passed. I pulled up a chair, took his hand, and, still not talking, just watched his face and wiped his tears as he poured out the misery and sorrow he and his family had gone through for the last few months as he suffered from the illness he had. It was so hard for me to leave him. I wanted to check back on him, help him with his problems, be there for him any way that I could. He said: "I haven't shared this with anyone; I don't know why I can with you," and those words which I have heard so many times before brought me back to the reality that it is my clown and not Karen that allowed him to be open with me. If I chose to stay with him, then the time I have for ministry outside my home is spent. There are other people who can take over now that my clown has allowed the words and feelings to flow from him and she can go on to other people. I hope that by seeing themselves reflected in the mask of the clown, they too will be able to shed their masks and allow themselves to be free.

The expression that has really come to have meaning for me since I began clown ministry is "the sacrament of the moment." I, of course, see God's wonderful creation at work in everyone I meet, but there are moments when my clown encounters another person when something magical happens. We both feel it. I know that God is right there with us. I know that the times I have to chase to meet other commitments, going home to do the wash, or staying next to the hospital bed or even times when the choices are not so obvious—that those moments are true sacraments and shouldn't be taken lightly.

I do have a commitment to my family. I want them to be at the top of my priority list. They, after all, are my first ministry, but they feel that they have their own ministry by allowing me to clown. My husband says that since he can't do what

I am doing and he really doesn't care to, then he can help by helping with my share of the home commitments and taking care of our children. Knowing this certainly helps me feel better when I have to choose how to spend my time.

Because I needed to supplement my husband's income and I wanted to use a skill I already had instead of going back to school, I decided to open my own clown business. Character Creations features different characters like the traditional holiday ones, except they are more than just a person in a costume; they actually become the character—for example, Mrs. Santa, Wanda the Wacky Witch, and the Easter Bunny. Because I believe that my ability is a gift from God to be used for his people, when I have an income earning job, I always stop by somewhere on my way home from work to play. As my business expands with new characters, so does my ministry.

I can't imagine my life now without some aspect of clown ministry. I get so much satisfaction from it. When I am in need of energy or laughter or when I am feeling lonely, I know that if I take my clown somewhere where someone else may be feeling the same, then I will come home with my needs met through the sharing. Many of my priorities of life have changed. I have found renewed interest in liturgy and the need to convey the Gospels in profound but simple ways. I have become aware of the homeless and hungry and now feel that I can no longer, as a Christian, sit comfortably in my modest home and ignore them. I visit nursing homes and look into old, lonely faces and see my own reflected there and know that something *must* be done to change our feelings that the elderly are useless to us and too great a burden. I have seen how people respond to my clown's touching and personal attention and so I allow myself to respond to that need when my clown mask is not on my face and it's just Karen, scared and vulnerable and needy, too.

Through this awareness it is becoming more evident to

me that if I am to have the time and energy to devote to clowning and the growth that has come from that, then I need to simplify my life and my needs.

My dream someday is to be able to strip away my clown mask and still be all that the clown represents. Until then as I grow from this ministry I thank God for allowing me to become a fool for him (1 Cor 4:10).

Matthew J. Hayes
Judy Hayes

Lay Ministry: A Couple View

Matt: It's crystal clear to me when I decided to become a "lay minister" (although I would have never recognized that term in those days). I had decided to leave the Jesuit novitiate at Milford, Ohio in early September 1967. The decision was very difficult—in those days folks still went to the seminary "for good." The difficulty was compounded by the fact that I had entered Milford only three weeks before—after a *huge* family send-off party that had even evoked the presence of our parish pastor (who had never been to our home before—or after!). The evening before I left Milford, I sat down and wrote about my new, and deeply felt, conviction that I didn't have to be an ordained celibate (in those days simply "a priest") in order to work on behalf of the Gospel.

My concrete inspirations for ministry as a lay person were found in some dedicated lay teachers at my high school who were role models of this possibility that ministry could happen outside of the realm of celibacy.

This decision was reinforced in my college years through the experiences that I had in a student group called Students for Christian Community. These experiences included periods of deep relationship building, times of retreat, and an increasing application of my Gospel beliefs to "political" choices being forced upon me by the Vietnam era draft.

96

During college years I met Judy. As we developed our relationship I found resonance, affirmation, and challenge for this growing desire to have my major life energy ("career") involve direct work on behalf of the Gospel. At the end of college, my goal focused upon teaching religion at the high school level—the only viable option known to me, as a layman, within the Catholic Church.

I attended the University of Chicago Divinity School, working toward a Ph.D. with the goal of teaching at the college level. During this period I became aware of the possibility of work as a parish director of religious education, an option which held greater attraction than teaching because it offered the possibility for work in a pastor/community setting (as opposed to being limited to the education/classroom setting).

So, as a lay minister I have moved through three years of high school religion teaching to work as a parish DRE (for four years). As I became more comfortable in the field of religious education as a DRE, I became aware of the importance of adult education as a means to enable the Catholic Church to become more deeply an "adult centered" Church.

I was able to widen the pastoral/community context of my work to include the *diocese* and became the Coordinator of Adult Catechesis for the archdiocese of Indianapolis. This context continues as I now serve as the Diocesan Director of Religious Education for the archdiocese of Indianapolis.

Judy: I married Matt—not a "career" lay minister in the Roman Catholic Church at the time—but a person who was (like myself) interested in a service profession, a profession that was meaningful in the sense that it was *for* and *with* people. Getting rich, getting ahead, becoming a success, were not goals for me; being happy and satisfied with the job that had an impact on people was.

Now after twelve years of marriage (eight of them as a lay minister's wife), I can say that his job as a lay minister has more than met my expectations. I feel it is an exciting time to be involved in ministry in the Catholic Church. We have found ourselves supported emotionally and spiritually by a parish in the diocese that has encouraged active involvement. I have seen Matt grow personally and professionally in these past twelve years. He is affirmed, happy, and challenged in his "chosen profession" and this has a positive effect on our family. I have also felt free and supported to pursue my own interests and "ministry."

Matt: I find my work meaningful for a number of reasons. Primarily, it offers me the opportunity to spend my energy and time on tasks and projects that are of primary concern to me. I am able to integrate my work with my beliefs and *strive* to live a lifestyle of Gospel integrity. Although I continually remind myself that my work doesn't really make too much of a difference, I perceive that my energies are spent in the service of building the Kingdom by working to move the Church (its people)—ever so slowly—toward maturity and adulthood. I also find my work meaningful because within it I find affirmation of my skills and talents, as well as opportunities for creativity and flexibility. My contacts with the faith communities within each parish are life-giving for me, as they are the occasion of signs of the continual presence and power of the risen Jesus.

Judy: Perhaps the greatest plus in the type of work that Matt has chosen is the immediate access to and involvement with a caring community of Christian people for our family. Our move to Indianapolis eight years ago was an easy one because of the parish that really welcomed us—providing us with practical information about doctors, housing, and schools, sharing lives and stories with us, and offering services and talents. I find after eight years that involvement in Church ministry is an invitation to a deeper sharing of all aspects of our lives with a community of people that are striving to live the

Gospel. From the very beginning, our relationships (at the parish and diocesan level) have been more than superficial.

Another plus was the person who actually "recruited" Matt to work at the diocesan level in religious education. She is a woman of high vision, who was extremely supportive offering an adequate salary/benefits to support a family, with deep sensitivity to the impact upon our family of the long hours and deep stresses that sometimes accompany work in religious education at the diocesan level. She was very much in touch with our family life and continually affirmed us as parents as well as "lay ministers."

Matt: I find the frustration within my work to be minimal. Like any full-time job, there are busy times and low moments when the tasks appear to be overwhelming. This especially happens when I'm "out in the field" (the archdiocese of Indianapolis covers thirty-nine counties of Indiana) for three to four evenings each week. Such a schedule takes a toll physically and psychologically—especially upon Judy who becomes, at these times, a "single parent" coping with three children under seven and working at her own part-time job.

There also are times when I become *intensely* aware—as a lay person—of the authoritative/hierarchical structure of the Roman Catholic Church that can stand in the way of individual and community growth at the parish and diocesan level. Even the term "shared responsibility" sometimes frustrates me because I wonder if, because of baptism, we should not be working from the reality of "co-responsibility." The former strikes me as quite compatible with a Church built upon adult-child relationships (the adult/cleric shares his responsibility with the child/layperson—who really has no responsibility in his/her own right), whereas, the latter resonates with a more adult-to-adult relationship. Fortunately, this frustration does not surface too often due to the fact that I infrequently encounter blatant clericalism, which may result from the fact

that I consciously do not seek out situations/parishes that seem
comfortable with the "adult/child pattern."

Judy: Perhaps the greatest frustration of Matt's work as a
lay minister has been his involvement with the *human* Church
(perhaps also his greatest strength). There are many times
when Matt's encounters with petty personality conflicts, politics, and power struggles take their toll upon my relationship
with him and the children. There is also the frustration of a
perceived lack of justice within the institution (e.g., what to do
about inactive priests?) This lack of justice is most deeply felt
in the area of salary for lay ministers: offering a living wage
that attracts and *sustains* a *family* person. Other frustrations
with Matt's work revolve around the irregular hours and the
weekend work, both of which increasingly impact on the family time as our children grow older. There is also a frustration
at certain times of the year when the work seems to be more intense, if not overwhelming. Upon reflection, there is also a
frustration about Matt having to "be available" to his constit-
uents many times without consulting about the impact of his
availability upon the family. I realize that this is no different
than the situation of many families where one of the parents is
pursuing a profession of service to the public.

Matt: I can still remember the first conversation that Judy
and I had in college about future plans about our "careers" and
the implications these had for our possible future lifestyles together. The memory of the conversation that remains is my
awareness that my "dream" (of working within the Church as
a lay person, with the obvious consequences of a limited income) seemed to resonate with her values. The "economic"
realities of working in religious education as a lay person and
being the primary financial support of a family with three children, dictate, I suppose, a "simpler lifestyle." We find this not
a hardship, but rather a benefit. We are less able to tie into the
consumer lifestyle that we witness among others of our cohort,

and we feel that this results in a healthier, more just mode of living. We are very conscious that our life is comfortable, that we live a more affluent life than the majority of our brothers and sisters in the world. Fortunately we have what we feel are essentials. We anticipate that the impact of consumerism will be more heavily felt as our children become adolescents, and hopefully that the economic "reality" of our lives then will call for a similar mode of living as now.

It would seem incongruous to us to have individual lay ministers within the Catholic Church receiving salaries/benefits that would make a "high consumer lifestyle" possible. This, to us, would be a contradiction of the values of the Gospel of which the Church is called to be a "sign and instrument." We have found ourselves a bit uncomfortable over the last four years as my salary has doubled (moving from parish to diocese). We have consciously tried to keep our spending patterns at the level of the earlier period, and have eased some of the discomfort by supporting others who were in financial situations that required assistance.

Judy: Matt's work as lay minister in the Church has certainly brought about a simpler lifestyle for our family. As I mentioned above it has brought us into continual contact with people who are consciously trying to live the Gospel. We find a continual tension between the radicalness of the Gospel and the desire (instilled in both of us by depression conscious parents) to live a "comfortable life."

In another sense our lifestyle has been growing more complex as Matt has moved from the parish to diocesan level. We have become increasingly more aware of issues and concerns that call for attention and action; we struggle with the complexity of these issues and their impact upon the activities and concerns that are fielded by a family of growing children.

Matt: I find increasing acceptance in my role as a lay minister in the church. When I joined the diocesan education staff four years ago, I was one of two lay persons among seven "professionals" (two priests, three sisters, two lay men). I now work with a team of eight (two sisters, five lay men, one lay woman). In the archdiocese of Indianapolis there is an increasing shortage of ordained ministers. As a lay minister with this local church I find increasing realism and genuine enthusiasm for my work. My status as a lay person, I feel, enhances my work with lay parishioners. I also perceive that the priests of the diocese tend to have more respect for the skills and talents of lay people who are pursuing a career (and support a family doing it) within the Church than they have for fellow priests, or religious sisters, in similar positions.

I have little doubt that the future of the American Catholic Church will depend largely upon the acceptance of a wider vision of eligibility for ordained ministry. This development will assist in the increased acceptance of the role of lay ministry alongside the role of ordained ministry.

Presenting My Entire Self to God

When I was eight, my parents, brother, sister and I moved into a company house in what we called a yard. Yard was an oil field term for those ten-acre lots where oil companies stored various kinds of pipe, enormous spools of winch line, and stacks of derrick parts. Our presence there was meant to be a deterrent to thieves. Three buildings stood in the yard: a big tin warehouse where my brother, sister and I played, the house in which we lived, and the privy down by the pipe racks.

We didn't attend any church. We seldom mentioned God.

I mention all this because I believe the roots of my ministry reach back through the years to that period in the yard.

One day my mother, who was dying slowly of cancer, taught me the Lord's Prayer. The words of the prayer fell on me like a song. Every night after I had successfully fought for slightly more than a third of the bed I shared with my sister and brother, I recited that prayer in an emotion of holiness.

When I was nine my mother died. Her final request was for Daddy to put all three of us kids in a Catholic boarding school. The day after the funeral, he did just that.

What an altogether different world! The nuns seemed ethereal with no flesh showing except the pale few inches of faces and fingers. Even more awesome was the chapel—that gaudy, glorious, blue and gold-leafed, statue-inhabited sanctuary smelling of incense and floor wax. How many nights, hanky-headed, I crept over its cool linoleum floor and knelt in dark wordlessness. Having never been in any church, I found this place wondrous.

In the boarding school we lined up to go to the refectory, we lined up to go to the classroom, we lined up to go to the chapel. Since we didn't line up to go to cry, I couldn't find a time or place for that. Consequently, I postponed grieving for my mother for about thirty years! That, too, has helped shape some of my ministry.

Besides the sisters, the chapel and the "lines," there were the boarders. Mind you, this was no fancy finishing-type school. It was a plain boarding school mostly populated with semi-orphans like us and the kids from what we called "broken homes." The boarders taught me what they had learned in their various schools of hard knocks. Let me assure you, it wasn't all piety! The yard may not have been a high class haven, but we had certainly been sheltered in its oily confines.

My heart still goes out in ministry to children like those children.

We worked for part of our tuition. My sister got to clean the music rooms. I, being older, worked in the kitchen. Every day after school I went to the kitchen and started my duties by peeling a tub of Irish potatoes. Sister Lillian (we called her Sister Lily) clicked her false teeth a lot and told marvelous stories about her home in Ireland. She became a sort of fearsome and kindly stepmother to me.

For a few months my Dad paid extra so we could have milk at meals. I felt uncomfortable about that because most of the kids didn't get milk. There was a definite distinction between the "working" boarders and the "paying" boarders, and my nine year old heart chose the former. To this day, I prefer working with poor and middle class people, and I still harbor a suspicion that the rich aren't quite as sterling as the poor.

In time I became a Catholic. I suppose my desire to serve in the Church formed gradually and unconsciously. If I had to pinpoint the time I felt *consciously* inspired to a life of ministry, I'd say it came one day in early adolescence when I read a novel entitled *White Fire*.

As literature, I imagine it was pitiful. It was a story about a nun who worked in a leper colony. She loved the afflicted people, especially a girl about my age who was ravaged by the "white fire" of leprosy. In response to the nun's prayer, God took the leprosy from the girl—and gave it to the nun. The girl felt bad about her friend and prayed to get it back. So the leprosy was tossed back and forth like a holy game of Hot Potato until finally the nun died and the girl left, cured.

When I finished that novel, I knew I wanted to serve people. This desire was complicated by the fact that I also wanted to marry. I struggled between these two futures.

I knew, of course, that they were mutually exclusive! I'd learned the catechism lesson. I knew that only men could choose the highest vocation. Women couldn't be priests, but they could choose one step above marriage by becoming a sister. Sisters could minister. Married women couldn't.

I entered the convent the summer after my junior year of high school.

In the seventeen years I spent as a sister, I ministered by teaching Theodore Dreiser and assorted literary company. I got a master's degree in literature and began to publish poetry, some articles, and my first book. I still consider the teaching of fine literature a service, and a significant part of my ministry today is done through publications.

Although teaching was satisfying to me, it fell short of white fire. As time passed and I wanted to engage in other

works, I became disillusioned with religious life as it was lived
then. I also became aware that, at the age of thirty-five I no
longer endorsed the commitment I had begun at seventeen.

Although I didn't want to be a sister anymore, my desire
to serve in the Church was still strong. Could I be lay and still
serve? I began to realize I could. And I have for the better part
of the last sixteen years.

My first job as a lay minister was that of pastoral assist-
ant. I had an old Dodge Dart that went on spontaneous honk-
ing sprees, a shabby furnished apartment, and a salary of $500
a month. I felt noble about my poverty and my low salary until
a jobless layman with a degree in religious education pointed
out that people like me kept people like him from being able to
work for the Church and support a family.

People in our parish seemed hungry for Scripture. At this
point I began graduate study in theology. Through Bible
study in the parish, I was able to do what I best knew how to
do—teach. More importantly, I was able to deepen my own
religious understanding and to find a lay style of prayer. I believe that no amount of skill and no number of degrees is sufficient to make a job into a ministry. Genuine lay ministry
must, I believe, be grounded in genuine prayer. Although people came eagerly to Scripture classes they didn't seem too interested in other courses and workshops unless those
workshops dealt with family life.

I quickly noticed that ordinary people seemed to be more
interested in learning how to rear an adolescent son, keep a
marriage healthy, or adjust to divorce than they were in, say,
learning about the early history of the Church. People in the
pews were also people in families. There—in kitchens and cars
and back yards—is where families live and that's where people
work out their salvation.

My parish work soon led me to full-time family-life ministry. I helped create and direct Oklahoma's first diocesan Of-

fice of Family Life. I went back to school and got a degree in counseling psychology.

In working with families, one of my most gratifying ministries involved working with widowed and divorced persons and with children who live with one parent. A good deal of this work was based on a program (The Beginning Experience) created by a friend of mine, Sister Josephine Stewart, S.S.N.N. In this ministry I helped people grapple head-on with their grief and begin to work through it. We emphasized that the only way *out* of grief is *through* it. The theological process on which this ministry is built is the pattern of pain-death-resurrection. People learn that the resurrection of Jesus is an *ongoing* power within them.

In the course of this ministry, I edited a book (*Learning To Live Again*) which includes the personal stories of two men and two women who faced grief and found within it the power of new life. I like to think that the book itself has become a ministry of sorts.

Since many of the divorced and widowed persons I worked with had children who were confused by the partial or total absence of parents, I very soon began helping the children. Those children came—and still come—before me like a parade of kids I knew in the boarding school. I'm sure that some of my special satisfaction in working with them also stems from my own childhood loss and the consequent empathy I have for children who lose a two-parent family through the death of a parent or divorce. I work with them and with their families in therapy, and I have co-authored a manual, *Children's Beginning Experience*.

In this regard, I find it fascinating to reflect on the ways God uses all these past experiences. Ministers (and isn't that every caring believer?) seem to seek to serve those who've had similar experiences. Social scientists might call it finishing unfinished business or doing vicarious emotional work. I suppose that's so. I also believe it's a kind of divine economy in which God moves us to use our own pain to help others. Perhaps only the wounded can really understand the similarly wounded.

Lately this divine economy has inspired a new emphasis in my ministry: working with stepfamilies. I married a man, Gene O'Brien, who was widowed. Gene has five daughters. My own experience as a stepmother inspired me to do a great deal of research and writing. I also work with stepfamilies in family therapy and in groups. Gene and I have created a program (*A Redeeming State*) to help couples prepare for remarriage.

Currently I work as coordinator of family life in a large inner-city parish. My work includes counseling and education. I find that some people more easily trust a counselor in a church setting than one in an agency. Some persons who come to me would probably not go for counseling at all if it weren't offered in the church. I sometimes pray *with* my clients, and I always pray *for* them. I make sure I don't substitute prayer for skill. I try simply to integrate the helping process so that it may accurately be named *counseling* and described as *pastoral*.

I believe that this particular ministry of professional pastoral counseling will be more keenly called for in the future. Priests are too scarce and too busy to add this time-consuming job to their schedules. Many of them lack professional training in counseling. Catholic parishes, at least in Oklahoma, are just beginning to see pastoral family counseling as a possible part of parish ministry. It's exciting to be in on the ground floor of this new and needed Church work.

As a lay minister, I generally feel well accepted by both laity and clergy. For one thing, people in Oklahoma know me. I've lived and worked here for the better part of fifty years, and although the Catholic population has shot up to four and a half percent, we're still few enough that many of us know each other. For another thing, this land of oil derricks and wheat fields is marked by a frontier spirit that sets an open and welcoming climate for just about anybody, including lay ministers.

Even here, however, the old taint of clericalism has caused some occasional frustration. I've been passed over for a diocesan leadership job because it "had" to be filled by a priest—even though I was better qualified by both experience and education. I've had to cancel a retreat because I had scheduled it to be held in some diocesan cabins used often for retreats. A notice from the chancery explained that lay persons (lay ministers) could not reserve the cabins.

Events like these infuriate me. What I find even more frustrating is the silence on the part of my clerical and lay friends about these kinds of injustices. That noxious idea that lay persons are inferior citizens in the Church seems still to linger among us. So, yes, I've experienced some frustrations as a lay minister.

In general, though, working in the Church has been good for me. I am instinctively religious, and I think God has given me the ability to make religion real and God personal to people who might be inclined to see religion as a Sunday event and God as an uninvolved overseer.

I find intense joy in helping children grieve when they need to, in helping single-again persons find new life, in helping stepparents give the lie to the Cinderella story, in helping couples improve communications and freshen love. I've found that Church work generally permits more creativity than non-Church work. I guess what pleases me most is that the work I do allows me to bring together my past and personal experiences and my professional skills. It's like presenting my entire self to God through service to God's people.

Megan McKenna

The Chicken-Littles, the Matches, and the Weasels

In the Book of Exodus the Israelites are caught at the edge of the Reed Sea. Before them the water, behind them the raging armies of the angry Egyptians. They panic and cry out against Moses and their God, Yahweh. And they are told not to fear—for the presence of the Lord is with them, in Moses, in the power that has been given to him as a gift and a service to the people. However, there is another piece of that story that isn't found in our Christian tradition—but is found in the rabbinic writings. One of the commentaries reveals that before God would part the Reed Sea, one Jew must find the courage to throw himself into the water. There is no magic.

The commentary is written in the present tense: one must find the courage to throw himself or herself in. It's the best image for the lay minister I've ever come across. Lay ministry is the anonymous personal gift of the life of an individual who reflects the power of God, the one who throws himself or herself into the chaos before the institution can make anything happen. One, or many, in the group must find the power, the strength, the courage and the grace to throw themselves forward into the sea of people, needs and the times. The gift, first of all, is the gift of a person into the lives of our community of believers. This is the reality of lay ministry: usually unrecognized, unacknowledged, half-believed in, non-validated, sometimes caught between a rock and a hard place, a place of exhilaration and surrender, surprise, miracles and endurance. It is a place of confusion and possibility, a place where one endures as much from one's Church and community as from the world. This ministry is not ordained, but it is charismatic, tightly bound in tradition and new forms. It is ministry that anyone can do; it is power enfleshed in just about anybody.

Lay ministry is a maturation and fulfillment of every Christian's baptism—the expression of faithful love and service to others that is tangible, noticeable, recognizable as a public manifestation of the believing community. In Matthew's Gospel we are told: "Go therefore and make disciples of all nations, telling them all that I have done and baptizing them." The lay minister's tasks are making disciples and telling all things, in any way possible. It is the role of the ordained minister and the believing community to baptize them in the name of the Father, the Son and the Spirit. So, most of the ministers of the Church are lay ministers—not known by title, not sealed in a sacrament besides baptism, not all that powerful, but they are the norm, the usual way of being Christian and nurturing and caring about the community, the faith and the world that needs believing persons and as much magic and mystery as it can muster.

THE BEATITUDES OF LAY MINISTRY

Blessed are the nobodies. In the past years I have discovered through ministers, people, some prophets, poets and children some of the ways of being that reveal what a lay minister is and does. The first is mirrored in the story of the Israelites and the unnamed Jew who took a risk. A nobody. Emily Dickinson has a marvelous poem; a few of the opening lines read: "I'm nobody. Who are you? I'm nobody too." This could be the refrain of lay ministers when asked "Who are you?" They are the nobodies with enormous power and possibility that most people don't even know are there working and making things happen by their lives, their beliefs and dreams and out-reach to others. This first beatitude introduces us to those who risk and throw themselves into the present moment and needs so that others may pass over and move onto the next stage of their journey.

Blessed are the compassionate ones. Those who do it with others. Together. They move, even if they stumble, and take someone with them. We are a pilgrim people, going home to-gether, and some folks find it hard to travel. Others need to see how we live with one another, whether it is ritualized in the communal reconciliation service, expressed in our teaching styles of team or apprenticeship, or revealed in action and re-flection practiced in groups that study the Scriptures, prepare the liturgy, work for justice or do hands-on-charity. There is always this commandment: Trust the folks; they are the lead-ers. Where they are, we need to be and we need to follow them everywhere until we catch up with them, and help them carry the baggage. Once again, the Christian community and the world needs to see "how they love one another." We go home together to our God.

Blessed are the tender lovers and the care-takers. Tend-erly, laughingly, with hope. Lay ministers take themselves lightly and others very seriously. They know a Christian is not allowed to despair. They preach a series of dance partners: death and resurrection; curse and blessing; sin and forgiveness; mourning and rejoicing. They always go hand-in-glove. Hope is their middle name. Hope and hang on until the morning star rises in the heavens. Unlike the disciples of Emmaus they don't give up and go off saying: "We had hoped he was the one." And if they do, they learn to backtrack fast, blushing at their own lack of faith and eager to share the news that God is

still with us and "has not left us orphans." The Psalms are sec-
ond-nature to them, for every emotion possible is a part of
their life, their prayer and their ministry. They endure. Life
with hope has carried them. And they return the favor by carrying others piggy-back for part of the way.

Blessed are the mindful ones and the translators. Most of
us live in our small worlds: families and friends, some community groups, our parish, the U.S. We are narrow-minded
without thinking about it, insulated, even isolated. Those who
are mindful open doors and minds, take down fences and build
bridges across prejudices, introducing us to the richness of
other cultures, languages, races and heritages. A lay minister
must speak another language: Spanish, French, Japanese,
Latin, philosophical or theological jargon. Which one almost
doesn't matter. We have two hands. One is for reaching out to
one we are comfortable with, one of our own people, and the
other is for reaching out for someone who is "foreign" or "al-
ien" or "just not yet known"—our neighbor. The mindful
ones, the translators make us aware that we are the universal
Church and that we must think of others at least as much as
ourselves. We are connected by baptism and by belief. We
must learn to be aware of others so that the world can see the
glory our God has left with us in the Kingdom. We need the
mindful ones to see beyond our noses and our local churches,
our building funds, to those in need, those struggling for justice and human dignity, our brothers and sisters who are poor,
and not yet comfortable in our land and presence.

Blessed are the justice-seekers. These are the ones who
are thorns in our side, who stick in our craws and keep hound-
ing us to make our belief a reality. They remind us of traditions in our faith that have sometimes gotten lost or forgotten
in the scramble of culture and domination: the documents on
justice, equality and peace, the new theologies of liberation
and freedom, the traditions of Our Lady of Guadalupe, the pa-

troness of the Americas who, as an Indian girl stands in solidarity with her people against the culture that brought a Christianity so overshadowed with violence and slavery that the new converts could barely see any justice or love. There are public ones: Gandhi, Berrigan, Dom Helder Camara, Thomas Merton, Dorothy Day and the ones who run the soup kitchens, the houses of hospitality, refuse to register for the draft or pay their military taxes, picket the nuclear weapons plants, write letters and keep bringing up the need for the churches to be involved in local politics and face the issues of abortion, ecology, welfare needs and the relationship between the Church and the State, here and around the world. These are the ones that say so clearly that we must hear: We are Christians, then Americans. Our first allegiance is to the Kingdom of peace and justice. These are the ones that Dan Berrigan describes ruefully when he says, "If you're going to work for justice, you'd better look good on wood."

Blessed are the humble-walkers with God. Simply. If you're a walker, you travel light, with only the bare necessities. These are the ones who reveal the Gospel to us by the way they live, who become in fact what we preach and teach. They protect our values and make us want to be poorer, live more simply, pare down our needs and rely on God and trust others who walk with us. They are careful of others' needs and weaknesses, careful of the world's resources, careful of others' talents and gifts, aware of "downward mobility" practiced by Jesus and Francis. They seek ways to live as children of God, include more people in our charmed circles, or, as Dorothy Day says: "Thank more and need less."

And this applies to our understanding of a minister as well. A lay minister does *not* have to be well schooled, only educated and experienced. The gifts are given to many more than those with the opportunity and advantages of a master's degree or academic credentials. Lay ministers are recognized and appreciated more by their lives and values and connections within the community and without rather than any set of initials before or after their names. The power of lay ministry comes from relation with the community and rootedness in God. It is simple, unadorned and ordinary.

Blessed are the witnesses. A man who epitomizes this act of witnessing is Elie Wiesel, the Jewish writer who makes the world remember the events of the holocaust. He tells the stories of the unknown ones, the survivors and those who died, the children, rabbis and the students—all the ones we often want to forget and can't if we are to retain some semblance of our integrity as human beings. These are the storytellers who tell the same stories over and over again. The ones in the Old and New Testaments and the testaments being written in our history today.

Stories and testaments like that of Tomas Borges, a leader in the Sandinista movement, a man who was tortured under the regime in Nicaragua. He watched his wife raped and tortured to death. He lived. He walked away limping, bent out of shape, blind in one eye, twisted but alive with those memories. After the victory celebration he met the man who had tortured him and his wife on the street. The general, terrified, pleaded for his life, or at least to be killed mercifully. Tomas went up to him, picked him up off his knees, embraced him and said: "This is my revenge. I forgive you." Testimony to the truth, to belief, to courage and the good news of forgiveness. Witness.

Or another newly discovered and shared story of Hannah Senesh, a young Hungarian Jew who worked with the underground in Yugoslavia against Hitler. She memorized the codes and radio frequencies of the resistance fighters and knew where the small groups were who were smuggling Jews out.

Captured, she was tortured in front of her mother and refused to reveal her knowledge to save both her friends and comrades and the unknown Jews escaping Hitler. She left us poetry and a life that witnesses to justice and freedom and the price of love unto death.

> Blessed is the match consumed
> in kindling flame.
> Blessed is the flame that burns
> in the secret fastness of the heart.
> Blessed is the heart with strength to stop
> its beating for honor's sake.
> Blessed is the match consumed
> in kindling flame.

She would have been twenty-three a few months after her death. Testimony comes from anyone. Lay ministers must stay close to these testimonies, to their people, and witness to belief, tell the stories, search them out. Every believer has a story to tell, a witness to make, and a life to share that makes the Kingdom come more quickly and brightly.

Lastly, blessed are the weasels, the single-hearted ones. Annie Dillard in her latest book, *Teaching a Stone To Talk*, in her first essay tells the story of a weasel, a creature so intent on one thing, that, no matter what, it would not let go after it had latched on. In this story, the weasel had bitten into the flesh of an eagle just as the eagle had buried its talons into the weasel for the kill. Months later the eagle was shot down, and buried still in the eagle's breast was the smooth whole skull of that weasel who hung on. She reflects on that weasel and wants to be that single-hearted, to hang on for dear life, "for a dearer life." And so, lay ministers can learn from the weasel, to find out what is the one most significant, passionate devotion of their lives. Grab for it and hang on no matter what—even if we are torn from earth by an eagle and lifted high above our usual ways and means. Blessed are the weasels.

These descriptions of lay ministers are very singular and peculiar—like the ministers themselves. They are beginners, novices always, half-finished theological statements, believers, your friends and neighbors, children, husbands and wives, lovers and prophets. Lay ministry isn't something new. It hasn't even changed much since the time of Jesus. It's always been there, the unwritten history and story of the Church. It's found in the Gospels where a young boy, daring to believe in Jesus' command to a hungry crowd and his disciples: "Feed them yourselves," comes and offers all he has to Jesus—a few fish and some loaves of homemade bread. His mother and family members were probably horrified at what he did, the public spectacle he made, the simple gesture of belief. That young boy and that unknown Jew who threw himself into the Reed Sea had a lot in common. They both believed and risked when many around them who were seeking to believe, even the disciples, didn't or couldn't risk.

A last story to wrap up the ordinariness and absolute craziness and hope of lay ministry. Once upon a time, Chicken Little heard that the world was coming to an end and that the sky would fall. He ran around, yelling and screaming in a panic. Finally in desperation, he ran out and lay down in the road and put his feet up into the air. After he had been there for a while, a soldier on a horse passed by the place and asked him, "Chicken Little, what are you doing lying in the road with your feet up in the air?" "Sir," he replied, "haven't you heard that the end of the world is coming and the sky is going to fall?" "Really now," the horseman answered. "You don't really think that your lying on the ground with your puny little feet in the air is going to keep the sky from falling, do you?" "Sir," Chicken Little replied seriously, "one does what one can. One does what one can."

And that is lay ministry, lying in the road and doing what one can. A Christian struggling to believe does what he or she can, and much to everyone's surprise, including the Christian's, it is enough, more than enough, and the Church is renewed, blessed and turned around again. It's no more difficult than walking on water (a la Peter) or sitting and watching by a tomb (like Magdalene) and being given the good news of resurrection because your need and love is so great. And it really doesn't matter if they don't believe you the first or second or umpteenth time you share that news with others. When you're "just a lay minister," there are no boundaries to what you can do, where you can go, except your own imagination and creativity, the community's needs and the Spirit's shove.

Blessed are all the Chicken Littles, the matches and the weasels, for they shall bring the Kingdom, reveal our God to us and delight our God again as once his child, Jesus, a carpenter, a story-teller and lay minister, did.

David Riley

Minister and Professional

My experience of being a lay minister in the Church perhaps can best be compared to the experience of a stormy love affair. It has been one filled with infatuation, disillusionment, anger, despair, acceptance, reconciliation, the entire range of emotions found in a love-hate relationship. It has been an experience of both amazing growth and incredible pain.

I have been employed by the Roman Catholic Church for about eleven years in different capacities relating to education. I was a teacher in parochial schools for three years, and I worked as a parish director of religious education for seven years in two parishes. This past year I was hired by my diocesan religious education office to work as a consultant to a number of parishes. I am thirty-four years old. I have a family, a wife and three children. Many times I have seriously considered leaving the employ of the institutional Church, but each time something always seems to happen to keep me going.

I think that something is the desire and the opportunity to share my faith with others, as others did with me when I needed it most. Somehow this sharing of faith happened either because of, or perhaps in spite of, the institutional Church. A community of people, a web of caring relationships, has always followed me to nourish my belief that indeed life does have meaning and purpose. Whenever I was plagued by questions of meaning there was someone there to show me the way, to tell me that I mattered, and sometimes even to celebrate that incredible truth.

My college years were searching years during which time I was not an active member of the Church. I was looking for a rational way to believe, a way to reconcile faith with reason. After I graduated and began teaching, I was persuaded by a friend to make a Cursillo weekend. I went, curious but skeptical. During the weekend I experienced a kind of love and concern that I had not thought possible in the Church. I did not find my rational way to faith but instead was persuaded to loosen my compulsive preoccupation with reason. Love has a way of convincing the mind, not through argument, but by overwhelming it. Something had to be real here.

Later on, when I decided to return to school full-time and study religious education, I found a language for my faith experiences, not in theology as one might expect, but through Jungian psychology. I discovered a new meaning for "symbol" and a new understanding of "myth" in both personal and collective forms. I began to understand religion from an experiential base. This opened the door for my return to the faith of my childhood, but no longer as a child. I did not so much believe as I *knew* because I had experienced. I began to relate my inner and outer experiences to the Christian myth. My own experiences became "funded" by the Christian story.

Gradually as my own conversion took shape and I could see the place from whence I had come spiritually, a growing desire developed in the direction of service. I began to see my life in terms of a commitment to help others to find faith. I wanted to be with others on their journey and to do what I could to help them find meaning as I had. I found myself wanting to give back some of what it seemed to me that I had been given, if you will, to love because I had first been loved. The power of my original faith experiences and the growing sense of a change in personal history, of truly being "turned around," impelled me to want to share that journey with others in the hope that they would be helped in their journey.

Fortunately my faith transition came at a time when I needed to make some career choices, and I was drawn through some relationships with faculty members in the religious education department at Notre Dame to seriously consider entering the graduate program. At this point my sense of ministry and my need for a career came together. When I received my master's degree I found a job teaching religion in a high school, and after a year I found myself wanting to get into parish work because it seemed more "pastoral." I really wanted to develop adult education programs, but I had little practical experience and there were few jobs in parishes for adult education coordinators.

One of those few jobs was in a large urban parish on the east coast, six hundred and fifty miles from our home. Out of my enthusiasm, idealism, and some sense of desperation at the prospect of being unemployed with two small children, we packed up and went. Thus we re-entered the mainstream of Church life and I became an adult religious education coordinator. My education had begun in earnest. I soon began to realize that there is a lot more to parish ministry than meets the eye, and I became skilled at making coffee and setting up chairs, but the real eye-opener was coming to the harsh realization that while adult education was priority number one for me, and, as far as I was concerned, for the Church, there were many adults who did not share that conviction. My job became one of convincing them of their need to be educated.

About the time I felt I had begun to make some inroads, the man who hired me was transferred to another parish. We were sent a young, progressive, middle-management type pastor. He had a somewhat different vision of my role, and my job description was broadened into that of parish religious education director. My responsibilities grew to include the entire religious education program. That meant more work for the same pay.

I must admit though, at first I did not mind the added load. My zeal and naiveté were so great that I had little concern for the cost and the benefits. Also the attitudes of parishioners became so much more positive. Things seemed so full of promise and new life under our new pastor. In retrospect I can see how my messianic visions of myself and the work to which I was utterly committed blinded me to what was really taking place in my own life. I was so absorbed in the parish life that I scarcely had a life of my own. I wanted to build the kind of caring community that I had experienced those years before, that had turned my life around.

In my blindness I inflicted much hurt not only on myself but on those I loved the most. While I struggled to build community in the parish and to exercise my ministry, my wife, Mary Beth, was at home with the children. She did not have the same relationships that I had and in a real sense I had developed a life apart from the family. The more I became immersed in that life, the more she felt a need to compensate for my absence by taking care of our home. I became more free while she became more trapped. I am convinced now that I was a true workaholic. I too was trapped in a kind of neurotic self-sustaining cycle. Because the needs in the parish were so great, and I wanted to meet them all, and there were no clearly defined criteria for success, I began to believe that if I just worked harder, somehow those needs would be met. But because of my lack of confidence and fear of failure, I would never let myself feel success. And there was no one that I could really turn to.

There was always the awful sense wherever I went that every parishioner I encountered was, in some sense, my employer. I felt as if I worked for all those people and that I had to make sure they were happy with me. I could not separate my "ministry" from my job. I could not distinguish what I did from who I was.

Things personally did not change much during my years of parish work. I tried to tell myself that I was doing better, that I was learning to delegate and let others take over. But I really felt that others could not do things quite as well as I. My tremendous need to save the Church finally came to a head last year when our marriage almost fractured. I know now that I was sick, and yet I felt powerless to change myself. I would always blame it on the work. And though the work was endless indeed, it was I who handled the demands so poorly. But in spite of my own weaknesses, there is another side to the story. My illness was not the only disease. It merely thrived in the presence of the Church's own structural sickness. That sickness grew as a whole new awareness and language of community, born out of Vatican II, pulled and tugged at the feudal structure of the institution.

Despite the development of lay ministry and some recent changes in canon law, most parishes remain choked at the grass-roots level. The pastor remains the dominant figure in the local church. As he goes, so goes the parish and lay ministry. I realize that twenty years is but the blink of an eye in the Church's evolution through history. But for us who live in this moment and work full-time for the Church, it is often no less a painful reality. Patience is difficult.

My experience with pastors has been that most of them are very fair men put in very unfair positions. Too much is asked of them. Expectations are more than most saints could handle. They are asked to be spiritual leaders, financial administrators, preachers, personnel managers, teachers, maintenance men. And since they are the focal point for everything, they experience a tremendous pressure to be all things to all people.

One thing that priests were never trained for is the role of employer. When I began working for the Church I assumed naturally that the Church would be at least as just an employer as your average corporation, and maybe better. I have come to realize that the Church has much more to say about ministry than about employment. The Church could, in fact, take a lesson from industry in employee relations.

Probably the most important expression of this issue for those of us who work full-time for the Church is that of salary. No matter how one couches the issue in the language of ministry and service, salary, in American culture, represents a statement about the value of one's work within a system. It is the bottom line, the acid test of justice when it comes to employment. We cannot escape it. This is particularly true for those of us who are trying to support families, whether lay or religious, who in a real sense also have a "family" to support.

Though it pains me, and it may seem obvious, I must say that in most cases the Church does not pay a just "family" wage. (A "family" wage as defined by John Paul II in his encyclical *Laborem Exercens* is a wage sufficient to support the members of a household without the other spouse having to work outside the home. The new Code of Canon Law urges Church leaders to pay a just family wage to Church employees.) An examination of figures from the Bureau of Labor Statistics indicating what is a necessary income for a family of four in various parts of the United States is very revealing when compared with what parish directors of religious education are actually making. The state of wages when compared to the community standard at even a modest level is truly pathetic. When I left parish work, my salary ranked in the top three percentile nationally according to figures found by Dr. Tom Walters in a recent study of parish DRE's. It was barely a living wage for us. I have known several DRE's who could not afford to live within the boundaries of the parish where they were employed.

The mistake I made was to accept a salary that I knew would create a hardship for my family. Sadly, I had a need to serve the Church more than it had a need for my services as expressed by what members of a particular parish were willing to pay for them. The capacity to rationalize and to make excuses for the Church is very great when one loves the work as I did. My regret is that I allowed that love to blind me to my primary commitment to my family's welfare, confident that the Church would, in the end, take care of us. On one occasion, my wife and I had to go to our pastor with a list of our expenses in order to convince him of our need for a raise. I should have left.

Many are doing just that. Until very recently the average life span of a director of religious education in a parish was one year. That seems to be changing a little, but the vast majority still are working under one year contracts. The exodus is particularly acute in married men, who when they reach the age of thirty-five often find that they can no longer afford to work for the Church. There is some strong evidence that their place is being taken by middle-aged women whose children are raised and who are not the main breadwinners of the family. Their husbands are making the money and thus the woman does not feel that she needs to ask for a salary anywhere near that of a married man with children. In fact she may even feel guilty for doing so. What seems to be happening then is the birth of a new class of lay minister: mature, inexpensive, and with the necessary free time to devote to an all-consuming job. It is not a consciously structured process, but a kind of ministerial natural selection that could eventually lead to the extinction of married men in professional ministry.

Aside from salary there were other aspects of and conditions surrounding my jobs with the Church that made it very difficult to remain. Thinking of my job solely as a ministry kept me going for a while, but as my children began to grow up, and my marriage began to crumble under the weight of countless evening meetings, I gradually came to the conclusion that I needed to also think of what I was doing as a job and to judge it with the criteria one uses to evaluate a job, because after all I was employed by the Church. I had to look at whether the job was ministering to me and my family. Was it life-giving?

On one level it was very fulfilling. I loved being a part of people's growth in their faith. But as a whole person, as a married man with a family, as a human being, I was dying. I have come to the conclusion that the main reason for the overwhelming struggle in parishes is that the role that I fulfilled, that of director of religious education, was so broad and undefined by the parish that it created impossible expectations both on my part and from parishioners. In most secular jobs, the work is somewhat defined within a context of the total work system. Roles complement one another for the accomplishment of the whole mission of the company. My job was like owning a restaurant and being the sole employee. When customers came in I was the waiter. When they ordered, I immediately ran to the kitchen and became the cook. Then I served the meal. When they left I became the dishwasher. Of course while I was doing these different tasks for one customer, the situation was complicated by the fact that other customers were continually arriving expecting service. It sounds like a bad dream. Unfortunately it was all too real for me and it continues to burn good people out over time. There was seldom, if ever, anyone around to say, "That's not your job."

I think that in parishes where parishioners do not take real responsibility for Church, many ministers take up the slack because their vision is so strong and so compelling that they cannot let it die. And so they become planner and implementer, supervisor and worker, everything from designing the program to setting up the chairs and making the coffee. But I learned that one-man or one-woman shows are doomed, and usually in the end they are not worth the trouble, because they are not products of an authentic process of being Church. It took me a very long time and much pain to begin to accept Church, and that meant accepting people, not for what I wanted them to be, but just for who they were. And it was only then that I began to love them.

But the need for affirmation in return, though it came in time from the people, is certainly not built into the job. I received many verbal strokes creating expectations on my part that they would be translated into things like salary and benefits. I kept thinking that in the end the Church would take care of such a valuable employee. Everyone expects to pay a lot for a new church roof or a new parking lot. They simply are fixed necessary costs. But the Church does not view its personnel in the same manner. The Church speaks very clearly and boldly in confronting corporate greed and anti-labor practices. But its own personnel practices and policies are strangely quiet, with an air of "You must be patient with us."

Probably the worst of it all is the feeling that in ministry one is all alone. There seemed to be no one who could understand what I was experiencing. I could not go to the parishioners, nor to members of the parish staff who were clergy since they were my employers. The system is structured in such a way that each parish is autonomous, making accountability and recourse very nebulous. Fortunately for many of us there are professional associations springing up in most dioceses, and they provide at least some support and solidarity for those who labor as "lone rangers" in the wild world of parish life.

Things are not all bleak. Slowly they are changing, as the Church gets more experience with lay ministry. Justice questions related to the employment of ministers are at least being talked about. In some places salary scales are emerging. Pension plans are being created, though they are small and do not extend in most cases beyond diocesan boundaries. That is, if a person leaves a diocese to work in another, he or she forfeits his or her pension. Medical insurance for ministers and their families is also becoming a part of employee benefit packages. These are tiny signs of hope that the Church as institution is beginning to learn a new ministry: that of employment. In the future, how well the Church learns that ministry will be critical to its very survival.

Most institutions learned it early in their lives. The Church is late of course because until recently it didn't need to know about fair personnel practices. Most of its ministerial personnel were not employed but vowed and ordained to obedience. Pastors didn't need to learn to be employers. What is happening is that not only are lay people beginning to demand just and fair personnel practices, but clergy and religious are also realizing that survival in ministry is more complicated than we used to think. People do need to be supported and affirmed in their work whether clergy or lay. It is a vital part of what makes up life and one's work.

One of those humanizing factors in any job is the chance for upward mobility. During this past year I had the good fortune to become a staff member in the Archdiocesan Office of Religious Education. This year has provided me with a completely new perspective on working for the Church. In many ways it has been a contrasting experience with that of parish work. I have found that many of the things that were painfully lacking at the parish level are present on the archdiocesan level.

The organization of the job is much better defined since the office operates out of a mission statement and written goals, objectives, and strategies. There is at least an internal sense of direction, and therefore a greater degree of teamwork on the part of the staff is often present, as well as a better system of accountability and performance evaluation. The feelings of isolation and aloneness have disappeared because of the encouragement, affirmation, and support of fellow staff and my supervisor.

On the whole I have found the system at the diocesan level is better managed and better paid, and that the job expectations are much more realistic. There is a decided awareness of personnel management principles, and there are policies in operation that help to clarify relationships between "labor" and "management."

I think the biggest change has resulted from the shift from what is largely an administrative role in the parish with all of the day to day details and pressures to more of a consultative role with indirect responsibility for the local parish. Along with the shift has come a sense of being once removed from "the action." But I think the change is psychically necessary. I don't think it is healthy to remain on the front lines for too long. This is borne out by some of the research in adult development that tells us that what a person needs and has to give to a job in early adulthood is different from his or her needs in middle adulthood. As a person gains experience he or she needs to be able to put that experience at the disposal of others who are in "the trenches." At some point the energy and enthusiasm of youth must give way to the acquired wisdom and patience of later life. There are currently very few opportunities in the ministerial job "system" for this kind of movement that recognizes adult developmental tasks. This holds true for clergy as well. When one becomes a pastor, what's left?

The Church today finds itself in a ministerial crisis, which in the root sense of the word is also an opportunity. One facet of the crisis is evidenced in the shortage of vocations to the priesthood. But I believe there is a much deeper and more serious crisis. Many individuals who are called to minister in the Church in a full-time capacity are finding the conditions under which they must labor intolerable. There is no real shortage in vocations. God is still calling people in great numbers. The crisis lies within the institution, within the structure. The forms of ministry created by the structure are not life-giving to those who must fit the forms. The needs of those who minister cannot be ignored.

Simultaneously, there is a tremendous burgeoning of lay ministry at the parish level, mostly in the form of volunteers who are no less called and no less needed than the professional Church worker.

But there will always be ministries which require special skills and training as well as a full-time commitment. I see a danger in not defining these ministries and what is required as preparation for them. The danger comes in confusing the two. Hence a pastor looks for a "warm body" to be his director of religious education. For too long in the Church we have been content to find someone who is willing but not necessarily able. The result is that we fill holes temporarily with someone ill-prepared to do an impossible job. There needs to be a distinction between roles that require professional full-time ministry and roles that do not.

It is impossible to summarize all of the lessons I have learned in working for the Church. Most of them have been painfully learned through many mistakes on my part. Others have come through the ways in which the Church has wronged me. Perhaps the greatest lesson which I am still learning is to try and forgive myself and the Church. Part of the healing process is to find ways of making meaning out of my experience. Sometimes that happens through finding an image or images that express one's story. A powerful image for me is that of the Good Shepherd in John 10.

Jesus, in trying to describe his relationship to his people, draws upon the ancient symbol to show how genuine and true is his love. It is such that he will gladly give his life for his sheep. He knows each one and they know him. There is a bond between himself and his sheep that is so strong that nothing can break it. In contrast Jesus points out the hired hand as one having no ownership of the sheep or interest in their welfare. When he sees trouble he runs, leaving the sheep to their plight. He does this because he works for pay; he does not work because he loves the sheep. He is only there to make a living for himself; he is not there for the good of others.

The obvious application of the image is that those who are called to minister must follow the example of Jesus in being good shepherds. They must have the welfare of others at heart, and if necessary in many ways be prepared to lay down their lives for their "sheep." The Church cannot be Church if it is run by hired hands. There is no place for the faint of heart who refuse to get their hands dirty with the stuff of human life.

This creates a tension that is acutely felt by those who work for the Church and must glean their livelihood from it. The tension that I have felt is precisely this: that the Church has variously asked me to be a good shepherd, but in many ways has treated me as a hired hand. When it came to dedication, loyalty, and commitment, I was expected to be the good shepherd. But when it came to salary, benefits, employee rights, etc., in other words, security, then I was expected to consider myself a hired hand. The Church in many ways has not been a good shepherd to me and to many of those like me. When we were in need of shepherding, of a measure of safety, the Church has often responded as a hired hand, fleeing from the responsibilities for stewardship of people.

For the reality is that unless the Church models, it cannot rightfully call. It cannot challenge others to the ideals of justice unless it at least is struggling to embody them itself. And that is why I believe that we are in the present crisis. There is a painful disparity between Church teaching on justice in labor and current Church policies.

I never wanted to be a hired hand, but seeing myself in that way, as someone who markets his skills in exchange for a wage, ironically, was necessary to my survival. In the absence of the Church, I learned to be the good shepherd to myself. The Church never taught me that. I still see my work as ministry, but I have come to terms with the fact that I cannot give my heart to it blindly. To do so is to have it broken again and again. I know now that it is not an either-or situation. I must become both minister and professional. To blur those distinctions destroys the necessary tension that must be maintained in working for and ministering in the Church. The challenge for me is to retain my vision, while at the same time respecting the reality of the Church today.

Sam Mackintosh

Interesting Times

"May you live in interesting times," runs an ancient Chinese curse. For me, the "interesting times" of the last quarter century have been as much blessing as curse.

When I was in college in the late 1950's Eisenhower was still president and Pius XII was, as they used to say, "gloriously reigning." It was the calm before the storm. During my senior year John Kennedy was preparing to run for president and John XXIII was elected Pope. The 1960's were about to begin—the Beatles, Vatican II, Vietnam. All hell was about to break loose in Church and society, the growing pains of a new world coming to be.

From my earliest years I have had two main concerns. One was to understand the world: "Why are things the way they are? Where did they come from? How did they get to be the way they are?" Both science and religion offer answers to such questions, so religion and science were my two great loves. I never saw science and religion as separate areas of knowledge, nor was I able to understand the opposition some people set up between them.

My second main concern was related to the first. Besides wanting to understand the world, I wanted to know how to respond to it: "What does one *do* with things? What is my place (my role or function or purpose) in the cosmic scheme?" These questions obviously are more explicitly religious. It was important to me not only to understand the world but to respond to it authentically. I had to be myself. (Once, in some program, I was asked to write an epitaph for my grave. I wrote: "He wanted to understand the world; he partially succeeded. He wanted to be true to himself; he wholly succeeded.")

I went to the Jesuit college in Philadelphia. In my senior year in high school I had been attracted by a recruiter's description of the required philosophy courses, especially his references to cosmology (the study of the nature of space and time).

For two and a half years I looked forward to the cosmology part of the philosophy course. When we finally got to it, the professor wasn't interested; he dealt with it superficially and I was disappointed.

But it was a minor disappointment. On the whole I was delighted with the education I received at St. Joseph's College. I ended up with about thirty (required) credits in philosophy and theology; I had several especially fine theology teachers, and received a solid background in the old theology as well as a substantial preview of the new. So Vatican II did not come as a surprise to me. With my understanding of the nature of the Church as "true but irrelevant" considerably altered, I was waiting for it. To me, it was long overdue.

Theology was exciting. I remember telling a friend from high school who had joined a seminary how exciting my theology courses were, and his response that I couldn't possibly be studying "real" theology because "everybody knows that theology is dull." Obviously, I was getting a better education in my Jesuit college than he was in his seminary.

I would like to have majored in theology. Of course, such a major was not available in those days, and in schools where it was available, it was intended only for seminarians. So I majored in science, my second love, and graduated with a B.S. in chemistry. I was also interested in other areas of science such

as astronomy, archeology and anthropology, and later earned
an M.A. in science at Wesleyan University.

With my love of knowledge and understanding, it seemed
natural that I should become a teacher. I earned a living as a
high school science teacher for eighteen years. During that
time I taught in three schools; all were Catholic.

I had learned a great deal about the nature of the Church
while in college, and when I heard, as Pius XII said, "We are
the Church," I believed it. I saw my work as a teacher in a
Catholic high school as my part of the work of the Church.
The term "lay apostle" was common in the 1950's; the current
"lay minister" doesn't seem to me much different.

I never thought of myself as a "lay minister" or "lay
teacher" or "lay apostle." The word "lay" seems to include
some kind of self-definition over against those who aren't
"lay"—i.e., priests. But I didn't see myself that way. The
words "priest" and "non-priest" were functional distinctions
that didn't seem to make much sense except in terms of who
"said Mass." I believed (and still do) that together "We are the
Church."

While I was in college I had discovered two important
thinkers: Teilhard de Chardin and C.G. Jung. Teilhard
helped me to see how my two great loves (religion and science)
fit together to make a perfect whole; Jung helped me to see
(among other things) the importance of symbolic ritual in religious experience. So with my education in science, philosophy
and theology, and what I had picked up on my own about their
interconnections (from Teilhard) and their expression (from
Jung), I had a fairly coherent picture of reality.

Sharing that vision of reality with my students was my
work as a high school teacher. If anything, I saw myself as a
"missionary," helping fulfill the mission of the Church. I was
helping to make the world better by educating young minds,
helping kids to stretch and grow to the maximum of their tal-

ents, helping them to bridge the gap between traditional institutional religion and the real world.

I was twenty-one when I began teaching; some of my older students were only four years younger than I was. So it was at the age of twenty-one that I had found my calling: "helping people to bridge the gap between religion and the real world." That is probably as good a description of my vocation as I can formulate. It describes accurately what I was doing during my eighteen years as a science teacher, and it describes just as accurately what I have been trying to do since then in the second half of my life.

In the first of the three schools where I taught, I was often in trouble with the school authorities for bringing up religious topics in science classes, and my efforts to organize religious study groups in students' homes were opposed by the principal. (The groups were highly successful; I still hear from some of the participants after twenty-five years.)

My second school was a fancy New England prep school. Neither the students nor administrators were interested in what I had to offer; I didn't stay long.

I remained at the third school for thirteen years. I arrived in the mid-1960's just as the crises of those years were breaking. Pope Paul VI spoke at the U.N. that year; I cut out his words: "No more war; war never again," from the banner headline in the NCR and hung them on the bulletin board in the front of my classroom. (With my science background, I had been aware of the dangers of radiation and nuclear war even before I began teaching, and always included discussions of those topics in my courses. I was an "anti-war activist," to use today's term, in my own way even back in 1959.) People were shocked that this new teacher had put such an "un-American" statement in a Catholic school—"and under the crucifix, yet!" said one of the many faculty members who came to see the bulletin board. But no one told me to take it down; they were, after all, the words of the Holy Father.

The school's ultraconservativism changed quickly as society exploded in those years of the late 1960's. Innovative teaching methods were introduced by an enlightened principal. I served as department chairman for about eight years and was able to do some creative work with curriculum (and with liturgy at the school, too, for a time; but the priests on the faculty soon put a stop to that). Perhaps the best thing I was able to accomplish was to organize and teach, for eight or nine years, a comprehensive science course from the cosmic perspectives of Teilhard de Chardin.

But the tides turned once again, and a new reactionary attitude set in. I was harassed by the newest principal (not, I'm sure, out of maliciousness; just sheer stupidity) and resigned as department chairman. A year later—exhausted from eighteen years of dealing with adolescents (most of it during chaotic social times) and from the lack of support from the school authorities—I ended my career as a high school teacher.

Thus began the second half of my life. Even before I left teaching things began to happen: several months before I marked my last exam new opportunities for ministry began to emerge and new paths became open to me for responding to my vocation of helping bridge the gap between religion and the world.

Because of my interest in Teilhard and Jung I was invited by the director to be part of the first group in a newly formed spirituality program at Wainwright House in Rye, New York. (Wainwright House is a former Protestant retreat center, now a focal point of the Human Potential Movement.) The new group, know as the Guild for Spiritual Guidance, was inspired by the work of Morton Kelsey; its purpose is to train qualified persons in the heritage of Christian spiritual direction, specifically in the context of the "new revelations available from the perspectives of Jung and Teilhard."

Much of the work I had been doing with high school students was in the nature of spiritual direction, helping them to bridge the gap between their personal lives and the traditional religious forms they had been brought up with. My first "call" to spiritual guidance had come when I was a senior in high school, and I was not a stranger to that ministry.

I had little money to pay for the program, but with some scholarship help and a generous gift from a friend, I became part of the first "class" at the Guild. A link was established between the Guild and New York Theological Seminary in New York City; combining my work at the Guild with my work at NYTS I was able to earn a Master's degree in pastoral ministry. In a credentials-conscious society, that degree has helped open doors which would otherwise have been shut to me. I made the two hundred mile round-trip "commute" from my home to Rye about fifty times over the course of the next two years.

While I have a natural gift for spiritual guidance, it is not, in my view, something for which one "hangs out a shingle." I'm happy to serve in this way, either formally on a regular basis or (more usually) informally, when people are led to seek me out. But it is not, and should not be in my view, something for which one is paid.

A second call to new forms of ministry came almost immediately after I stopped teaching. My interest in ritual and liturgy had led me to be of help to the pastor of an inner city parish in Camden, New Jersey, on an occasional basis. I earlier had organized an Easter Vigil service (somewhat unorthodox, combining the best elements of the Roman Vigil with those of the Byzantine Easter service and incorporating some work done on the vigil at Princeton a dozen years ago) as well as occasional feast day services. (The Vigil, now ten years old, has stood the test of time well. It begins at 4 A.M.; people often drive many hours through the night to be part of it.)

Once I had left teaching, the pastor asked me to give one day a week to work on the Sunday liturgy. I said I would. The inner city is poor in many ways, with poverty of talent and resources as well as of finances. I ended up putting into that effort what seemed to be about ten days of work per week.

When I began, perhaps fifty people attended the main Mass on Sunday. As the liturgy began to take shape and touch people's hearts, the numbers increased. Now, several years later, five or six times the original number are present regularly. On special days like Pentecost or Palm Sunday, the large church is filled.

Many who attend weekly do not live in the city; they drive in on Sundays, often from considerable distances. And they often return during the week to be of help in various ways. Part of the idea is that parishes not in the inner city can help those that are poor by sending people to help, to be part of the inner city parish. Most who come from a distance are not "commissioned" by their local parish; they have made the move on their own, a definite growing, and I think welcomed, trend in the life of inner city parishes.

There is no question that good things have happened as a result of my work with liturgy at the parish. But it has not been without its problems.

When I began, I was given total responsibility by the pastor, but absolutely no organizational structure to work within. Organization is difficult to come by when the daily crises and emergencies of inner city life take up the time and energy of the parish staff. As more and more people began to take active roles in the liturgy, communication became increasingly difficult. After three years, about sixty-five people were actively involved in liturgical ministry of some sort, all for the one Sunday Mass at 10:30. Without some structure, communication was impossible.

To deal with the problem, a planning group for liturgy was established. Now there was structure, but I no longer had a responsible position of authority. I was jokingly promoted from "director of liturgy" to "director emeritus." Officially I was to be a "liturgy resource person," but my role became that of negative critic; it was a frustrating situation. I had promised the pastor to remain with the liturgy group for one year, which I did, but I "retired" at the earliest possible date when the year was up.

Meanwhile, the new life given to the dying parish by quality liturgy had led to a new stage of development in the parish's life. Christian worship, once it becomes authentic, naturally spills over into service or ministry; people who gather joyfully around the table of the Lord on the Lord's day cannot but help see themselves called to serve those in need. In the inner city, the needs are great and the opportunities for service inexhaustible.

To help with this next stage in the parish's life, we set up a Lenten lecture-discussion series. The pastor presented two talks on the history of the one hundred year old parish in the context of the history of the city and of the wider history of Church and society. I presented two on the post-Vatican II models of the Church and on the basis for ministry in ecclesiology, baptism and the Eucharist (based mostly on Avery Dulles' work, some things from Karl Rahner and from the liturgist Ralph Keifer). The final evening was devoted to the present state of ministry in the parish: what was being done well, what poorly, what not at all. The Lenten series led to an all-day meeting of the parish (we called it our "synod"), held near Pentecost, in which nearly one hundred parishioners discussed what it would mean for them to offer prophetic service as a sign of hope in the city and how they might organize themselves to fulfill that mission. Responsibility for ministry was effectively put into the hands of the parishioners. "Lay" ministry had been taken seriously; the parish was coming of age.

My present position in the parish is something like "consultant for liturgy and ministry." Recently I was asked to serve as a "consultant" along similar lines for two parishes in Philadelphia.

Yet a third opportunity to respond to my vocation of bridging the gap between religion and everyday life came soon after I left teaching. For a long time I had wanted to share with other parents what my wife and I had experienced, along with our children and friends, of the joys of family religious celebrations in our home. My interest in the ritual celebration of feasts and seasons in family life flows naturally from my concern for liturgy; it is a major aspect of my early concern about how to "respond" to reality. It is also the only real hope for the long-range improvement of our public worship. As Msgr. Balthalsar Fischer, *peritus* at Vatican II and framer of the Council's *Constitution on the Liturgy*, has said repeatedly, "The liturgy will have been renewed in the Church only when it has been renewed in the family."

So in July 1978 I began publishing a small monthly newsletter dealing with family ritual. I called it *Greenblade*, from the old Easter hymn which sings of the green blade rising from the buried grain: "Love lives again, that with the dead hath been; Love is come again, like wheat that springeth green." The image is one of fragile life emerging from the earth after being buried and thought dead; it's a good image for the rediscovery of the symbolic life currently happening in our society. I saw *Greenblade* playing some small part in the restoration of the experience of the sacred in everyday life, an experience which has been obscured in recent times by our bewitchment with technology and by the dust of the centuries which had accumulated in our overly-institutionalized Church.

Greenblade appeared monthly for two and a half years. In the meantime, the publisher at Resource Publications, Inc. in San Jose, California saw some issues and asked if I would consider editing a magazine along similar lines. That was the beginning of *Family Festivals* magazine. The first issue appeared in August 1981; its present circulation is well over 10,000 and growing. Response from parents throughout the country has been gratifying.

I like to think of *Family Festivals* more as an attitude or a "spirituality" than simply as a publication. Its purpose is to establish a sharing network of what families can do and are doing to nurture the symbolic life within the home and to help their children experience the presence of God in their everyday lives through ritual celebrations.

A fourth area of my ministry is writing and teaching. I teach part-time in the theology department of my old alma mater (now St. Joseph's University), and give workshops, talks and conferences for various parishes and diocesan organizations. My university courses deal mainly with the fundamentals of religious experience found in the religions of the world and the way those basics of human experience find expression in the Christian tradition. My diocesan and parish-sponsored talks and workshops usually focus on the theory and practice of family celebrations.

I also write, mostly about religious ritual, in either its public (liturgical) or private (family) forms. I've done some things for The Liturgical Conference in Washington and for Chicago's Liturgy Training Program. I created a unique liturgical calendar for LTP, a colorful poster calendar which shows the feasts and seasons of the year at a glance; it's now in its third edition and I see it in a surprising number of classrooms and homes as well as liturgy committee meeting rooms. I also do a family column for a local Catholic newspaper and some of my articles have been published in *Sacred Signs*. A few odds and ends have appeared in other author's books, either as extensive quotes or, in one case, as an appendix. I'm currently working on several articles for Paulist Press.

I also write the liturgy review column, under the pen name H.E. Geria, for the Delaware Valley's *Catholic Voice*. Once a month I attend Sunday Mass in a parish in the area, usually one suggested by parishioners; I then review that liturgy in the column in the same way a restaurant critic reviews the quality of the food, service and atmosphere of a restaurant.

As you might guess, the column caused quite a bit of fuss when it first appeared. Some readers objected that the Mass should never be criticized. "The Mass is the Mass is the Mass, no matter how it is said," they felt—ignoring the pleas of Popes, bishops and ordinary people over the last few decades. Others, mostly pastors, just didn't like being held publicly accountable for the quality of the worship available in their churches. Many readers were delighted with the column.

From my encounters with Catholic parents all over the country, I have learned that the most burning religious issue for them is not a theoretical one like papal infallibility or women's ordination. It is, rather, the very practical concern: "Where can my family take part in a reverent, dynamic, alive Sunday Mass?" They complain over and over about the dull, lifeless services available to them and cry out for authentic worship. So I see the liturgy review column as a service on behalf of all who hunger for living worship for themselves and their children; it is one more way of helping bridge the gap between institutional religion and real life.

From all this work—*Family Festivals*, mini-conferences, liturgy workshops, teaching, editing and writing—my income is about half of what is needed to support my family. My wife's income supplies the rest, but together our total income is such that we must live simply. We are, by government standards, poor.

Small is beautiful, but poverty is not. A minimal income is highly inconvenient. Our thirteen year old car, for example, may break down at any moment. The inconvenience bothers my wife (who writes the checks) more than it bothers me, but we both must remind ourselves frequently that secular society need not define for us our understanding of "success."

It is frustrating that the parish where I work can not afford to pay me adequately, that the local diocese will not hire me to do the work I might, or that there is not yet sufficient institutional support for *Family Festivals* magazine that I might give myself full time to that work.

And yet my life is so rich in so many ways that I can truthfully say along with St. Paul that "having nothing, I possess all things."

But my work is too scattered. I am pulled in too many directions at one time. I would like to have just one, or at most two, major responsibilities, each of which would pay adequately so that I might give it full attention. In one day I may go from lecturing university students in the morning on Karl Rahner's idea of God to speaking in the evening for a group of non-church-going parents whose children are making First Communion, and, in between, giving many hours of attention to details of liturgy planning, proofreading, checking mockups, revising manuscripts, conferring with authors and planning future issues.

One important advantage of all this is that, because I can do much of the work at home, my kids probably see more of me than most kids see of their fathers. But I was moved to tears at the Twelfth Annual Conference of Notre Dame's Center for Pastoral Liturgy when Fr. Robert Hovda spoke of the plight of persons like myself who, because of unfair economic practices in the American Church, often find themselves "unable to distinguish between their response to a vocation and their instinct for survival." Indeed. It is not easy to avoid bitterness.

Have I been accepted as a "lay minister"? Primarily because I do not think of myself as a "lay" minister, I think I have not. I see myself—and hope that others see me—as someone who is doing what he feels called to do.

I think "lay minister" is a term used mostly by people who see themselves as doing "Church work" for a living; if they are not priests they must be "lay" ministers. Lay people who aren't ministers don't think much in terms of "Church work" and "non-Church work"; it's only lay people who are involved in it who do.

My need is to be myself, and that means doing what I have to do in response to my vocation. But I do it as me, Sam Mackintosh, and not with any sense of myself as "non-priest." I think it is my calling to help bridge the gap between the institutional Church and everyday life that keeps me from thinking of myself or anyone else as a "lay" minister. The term is itself indicative that the gap remains to be bridged.

Do people understand what I am doing? For the most part, I think not. While "bridging the gap between religion and life" has been the essence of my work during both my high school teaching days and now, the former work had a clear focus. Everybody knows what a teacher is. But my present work centers on religious ritual, and few have much understanding of that. "Editor" has some meaning for most people; even "director of liturgy" makes sense to educated Catholics nowadays. But being a person who earns a living by dealing with the principles and practices of symbolic ritual—that makes little sense to anyone.

I think I understand why. In our culture, due to the overemphasis on technology and science in the last few centuries, the non-verbal right-brain mode of human activity—what

C.G. Jung calls the *intuitive function* of our minds—has been undervalued. Even our use of the word "intuition" is mostly negative, as in the double put down, "women's intuition." We seem to have been hypnotized—literally put into some kind of trance—by logic, by our ability to make verbal distinctions, and by the control that technology gives us over our world. We have lost touch with a basic part of our personality, and it is precisely the part through which we worship. Liturgy, religious ritual and celebration operate essentially out of the non-verbal, intuitive, right-brain part of ourselves.

Americans, and Westerners generally, seem to be afraid of that right-brain intutive function. It is closest to the unconscious world—a world as vast as the cosmos outside ourselves—and it is frightening to many. So we have yet to discover that it is primarily through the intuitive function that we come to God, that we experience the sacred presence and receive healing. We do not yet realize that worship is not another form of technology where we try to control the world or God. Worship is different. In worship we "hold hands with the universe and sing."

I often wonder whether the great stress on an intellectual approach to worship, so often promoted by religious educators, with its unrelenting attention to "themes," isn't a more or less intentional, although unreflective, attempt to keep God at a distance—precisely in the same way that persons who focus on the presence of Christ in the tabernacle keep themselves from being able to accept his presence in their hearts and in the hearts of the community at worship. Far fewer demands need to be made on oneself that way.

But good things are happening in this area of ritual and celebration and I seem to have some small part in it. It is exhilarating to be part of the growing edge of Church and society, to be plowing new ground and helping in a small way to bring the Church to maturity.

And even if it is difficult for people to understand what I am doing, I know that the results of my work are a delight to many. Jesus says, "By their fruits you shall know them." The fruits of my work are accepted well.

There are persons who will never be the same again, who are "eternally wounded," as a poet says, because of my work. When I am told, by an old woman, poor and sick, that "I stay alive only to come to this Mass on Sundays," I know that my liturgy work has meaning. When, following a parish seder and Eucharist on Holy Thursday evening, the results of my efforts, a poor old man in his eighties says, "This was the best night of my whole life," I have no doubt that my work is meaningful. When a parent says to me at the end of a talk, "I have discovered a new vocation in life because of what you said today," I know my efforts are significant.

Jesus also says that his "yoke is easy" and his "burden light," but I have little experience of that. I often get discouraged and wish I could "give it all up" for a nice secure 9 to 5 job. I often think of Dorothy Day who founded the Catholic Worker movement along with Peter Maurin and became the American Church's social conscience for half a century. Once, in a "down" moment, she said of Peter, "I wish to hell I had never met him." I know how she felt.

Sometimes I see more clearly. At those times I have no doubt that the world is different and better because of the work I have been doing over the last twenty-five years. It's then that I know that the "interesting times" we live in have indeed been, for me, far more blessing than curse.

Patricia Livingston

Lay Ministry:
Poetry and Truth

The ruby light of a sanctuary lamp would flicker by a tabernacle, giving off a gentle beeswax scent. A crucifix hanging over an altar would throw the shadow of a long cross on a wall. A slight creak from a wooden kneeler or the soft rattle of a rosary against an oak pew would only heighten the thorough, holy stillness.

It was here—a whole series of heres—in my parish church, in the Sacred Heart Convent school, in the tiny chapel in the dorm at Trinity, that I experienced a summoning of the Spirit.

Ministry begins with a call to serve. For me the inner call happened in those times of prayer, beginning about twenty-five years ago.

Ministry, however, also requires an outer call. It is a designation, an authorization within the community of the Church, to perform some special function, to accomplish some purpose that serves the Kingdom. The inner and the outer call must be heard and accepted.

It is only in the last five years that all of those things have come together for me: the inner call of the Spirit, the outer call of the Church, and my ability to accept. Since then I have been doing it as a life work.

My ministry involves teaching and counseling. I travel

148

and give workshops and lectures about various human things: about communication and relationships and sexuality and stress and play; about dealing with conflict and caring for yourself and ways to love perhaps a little more easily. The central focus of it all is the call to the Kingdom, the call to oneness with each other in the Father, and the call to union within ourselves.

I work primarily with priests, but also with women and men religious and with lay people.

When I was invited to write this chapter I reflected for some time on my experience of lay ministry, and I was struck by how significant it has been that it took so long for the inner call, the outer call, and the ability to accept to come together. In that twenty years my perspective on ministry changed radically. I am choosing for the focus of this chapter the story of how that change occurred, and why it was crucial to my ability to be a minister.

When I first thought I was ready to do it, in college, it was called the lay apostolate. I belonged to an organization called Sodality; I had shining idealism, limitless rose-colored energy, and hope no shadow had touched.

That was a time of great security and positive expectation—the Eisenhower era. I was at the heart of it. I even went to Ike's inaugural parade.

It was the pre-Vatican II Church, a bastion of the ideal and the safe. We prayed at the foot of the altar after Mass for the conversion of Russia, and we knew that it would happen. There were clear, certain dogmas to believe and laws to obey to get to heaven.

We had a book, I remember, called *The Question Box*. In it were all the possible questions that non-Catholics might ask, and the correct answers to each of them. I tried to learn them all.

I made the nine First Fridays five different times, and I

tried to recite perfect acts of contrition at night. I worked on my spiritual progress by concentrating in a "particular examen" on a certain sin or fault, trying to eliminate it from my character.

The prevailing philosophy seemed to be conversion to the ideal: Catholicism, democracy, perfection. It was a wonderful time to grow up. Everything was in order: protected, predictable, polite.

Responsibility was also part of it, however. Those with faith, with truth, with education, needed to be aware that this was not for them alone, but was to share. To use for the Church. To bring others to faith, to perfection. A motto I heard repeated was: Noblesse Oblige. Nobility has obligation. To whom much is given, much is expected.

In that spirit I memorized and said daily the prayer of St. Ignatius:

> Dearest Lord, teach me to be generous;
> Teach me to serve you as you deserve:
> To give and not to count the cost,
> To fight and not to heed the wounds,
> To toil and not to seek for rest,
> To labor and not ask for reward
> Save that of knowing I am doing your will.

There is great beauty for me in the memories of those days: the innocence, the simplicity, the fervor.

But I now understand why I was not given a chance to be in ministry, as I so longed to do. I did not yet understand the Real. I had not come to terms with my humanity.

John Dunne, in *The Way of All the Earth*, writes about poetry and truth. He quotes Goethe's autobiography: "It is good to turn the truth of one's life into poetry, but very destructive to try making poetry come true in one's life."

Dunne gives the example of Cervantes' Don Quixote, "the satirical portrait of a country gentleman who, crazed by his reading of books of chivalry, sallies forth to make poetry come true."

At the time of the height of my idealism I married a strong, handsome Knight of the Hudson, a West Point second lieutenant, and set about making life out of the poetry of the Church and the era. It turned out that the world of the 82nd Airborne Division at Fort Bragg was on a different map altogether from The Land of the Perfect and Polite. Again and again the windmill I was tilting with would knock me off my horse. My vision kept being challenged.

A strong example was when I had my first child. Pregnancy had been vastly more troublesome and painful than I had ever imagined, and I was well into the tenth month, something I didn't know could happen.

I had prepared for the experience of delivery, planning how I would offer up the labor by the hour for different intentions: the conversion of Russia, the missionaries in China, the souls in purgatory. Somewhere after about the fourth hour all thoughts of offered-up-intentions disappeared, and I got lost for the first time in my life in fear and pain. I could hear other women moaning and screaming up and down the hall. I was on an island in a sea of red that enveloped me and receded, but never far. All the pious images I had read about suffering broke into little pieces, and I knew for certain and forever that they had not been written by anyone in pain.

Women came and went in the semi-private labor room with me, and the hours crawled on. One of them was a black woman who was having her fifth baby, and who said she hoped it was a boy because she had four girls. She looked at me with compassion, saying, "This is your first, isn't it, honey, and you're a long way from home." I couldn't believe there was that much kindness in the whole world.

She worked with me then, telling me how to breathe and what to do. At one point she said: "Now, honey, I'm going to be gone for a while, but I'll be back. My baby's coming." Her baby! I hadn't even noticed, I was so lost in my own struggle. She did come back, smiling. She had a fine strong boy, named for his father. She kept helping me until she told me to ring for the nurse, that I was getting close. When I came back, exhausted from giving birth to an exquisite little girl, she was gone.

In my epic poem, the heroine offered pain for others. In my experience of life, she got lost in it, and desperately needed help from someone else.

About six months later, I learned I was pregnant again. My due date was in the middle of Lent. Again, I had an ideal vision I tried to make true, deciding what I would offer. It could be another extended pregnancy, a prolonged labor, a difficult delivery. That is what I would offer to God for the people of the Church.

When it happened, I entered the hospital a week early. The labor was brief, the delivery was easy. But my baby was stillborn. I had decided what I was willing to offer to life. And life decided to take my son.

Gradually I let go of trying to make the poem come true, and tried just to accept the days that came. There were two more babies very soon, two strong sons. There were many moves back and forth across the country. There was the infinitely humbling, stretching experience of being a wife and mother, and finally the anguish when the marriage between two good people who were drastically, utterly different ended. That was certainly not in the poetry.

I was face to face with my own humanity. I found, unlike Ignatius, who was more of a seasoned fighter than I was, that I *had* to count the cost, or I would lose myself. I *had* to heed the wounds or I would bleed to death. I came to know my limitations, my doubts, my anger, and the deep shadows on my hope.

In the years that followed, there was a person who came into my life who crystalized my awareness of my own poverty, who became, against my will, so much a part of my daily life, that I was forced to see in her humanity the symbol of my own being.

She was old, very old. She had come to this country as a kind of mail order bride for a German man who wanted to settle in the wilds of Florida. When there was nothing there but swamp mosquitoes and huge snakes, she farmed with him and bore his children and worked until his strength gave out, and then worked on alone.

When I first began to see her she could no longer work, but she would walk, rocking from side to side along the road, her knees stiff. She would cover about ten miles in a day, picking up cans from the side of the road, and going through trash cans for usable food.

Her face was tough and brown and folded in on itself from decades of Florida's endless summers. Hair grew from her chin, and most of her teeth were missing. She wore layers of clothing and long wool stockings even on the hottest days. Her smell was very strong.

She began stopping at my house to see if I had anything I didn't want. I offered her something to drink, and then something to eat, and she ate with a kind of greed whatever I had.

She started coming almost every day, and then, as her memory got worse, more than once a day. I got so I really dreaded it. I was terribly busy working and raising the children. I became increasingly repulsed by her, by the odor, the sack of garbage, the demanding aura of neediness.

I felt terrible that I resented her, and I would try to welcome her as the Lord in the guise of the least of his sisters, offering her food and drink and time in his name. As she ate I would try to send her a blessing, to imagine a blessing, gentle and deep, going to the heart within her wizened body, trying to touch the beauty within her and bless it.

One day an extraordinary thing happened. I had been silently trying to give her a blessing. As I looked in her clouded blue eyes, suddenly I was aware that there was coming back to me from her a blessing, also gentle, also deep, as if the God-presence, the beauty, the soul of her, was offering me grace.

At that moment I knew that we were one. Both of us were beggar and lady. She was what I fear most for myself: not only not to be perfect, but to be desperately, greedily needy. Right there in the chair across from mine was personified that side of myself I found it so hard to admit to the table of my consciousness. I had struggled with letting her into my home again and again until I saw it clearly. I too am hungry, ugly, lonely, weary, afraid. When I hide that from myself, it can take me over. When I try to acknowledge it, to seat it at the table, when I give it my blessing, it blesses me in return.

Soon after that she stopped coming. I heard conflicting stories about what had happened to her and never really knew for sure. Perhaps she stopped coming because she had finally been able to give me her gift. Her blessing had been received.

I once thought the goal of spiritual life was perfection. I worked on it systematically, and was hard on myself for failure. I had a holy card in my missal that said: "Be perfect as your heavenly Father is perfect."

I recently learned from a priest friend of mine that scholars now think that passage was written later, and is probably not as close to what Jesus actually said as is the passage in Luke: "Be merciful as your heavenly Father is merciful."

In the exchange with the old German woman, it came with great force to me that not only did she need mercy, but I need mercy. Being human is not being perfect; it is being imperfect.

My understanding of the human person has been greatly enriched by the teaching of Carl Jung that the goal of life is wholeness. To become whole means not only the developing of strengths, but the recognizing of weakness; not only becoming The Best I Can Be, but also acknowledging The Least of These My Brethren within me. Denying my darker side does not make it go away; it only shuts it off where it gathers power and undermines the best of intentions, turning into a crone going through garbage because of hungers I won't recognize.

If I had gone into ministry in the early 1960's, I would have fallen into the trap that comes from not knowing my own dark side. It would have been only the *others* who were poor.

If I refuse to acknowledge my own needs, I project them on others. I am then too identified with the people I minister to, and I tend to "over-help" or "rescue" them, doing for them not only what they cannot manage, but also what they need to do for themselves. Like an over-protective mother, I support their dependence.

If I don't admit my own hungers and requirements for rest and nurture and friends and inspiration and learning, I tend only to give credit to the needs of others. It is very hard for me to say "no," to assert, to define my boundaries. I tend to neglect myself and burn out.

If I refuse to realize that my own imperfections are part of the mixed quality of my humanity, I become terribly sensitive to criticism and feel enormously ashamed at each small mistake or inappropriateness. Or I may stick to what is totally safe so there will be no danger of experiencing failure or rejection or error.

The young woman kneeling in the cross-shadowed, candle-lit stillness of a chapel in the early 1960's praying to be allowed to minister was not ready. She did not need to learn more about perfection; she needed to know more about being human.

Within a month of the last visit from the old woman that so confronted me with my own humanity, the call to ministry came. It was the outer call of the community of the Church asking me to begin teaching seminarians and priests. It came in the form of three calls very close together in time: one from Fr. Frank McNulty of the Darlington Seminary of the archdiocese of Newark, one from Fr. Vincent Dwyer of the Ministry to Priests Program, and one from Fr. Robert Pelton of the Notre Dame Clergy Institute.

Deciding whether to accept the call took careful discernment and prayer. It meant giving up my school system job and taking the risk that there would be enough work to support myself with the children. I tried to listen for the inner call. I said yes.

It has been five years now, and I have been with many different groups. The focus of my work is not perfecting, but heartening. People who come to me for counseling or take my workshops are usually coming because they—like me—have found that poetry is not easily made into truth. They have encountered the less-than-perfect human condition, the Real, and are looking for skills and insight and encouragement.

The essence of my ministry is an attempt to articulate the human experience, and to enable others to do that for themselves, hoping that this will put them in touch with their own hearts, and will empower them to recognize with mercy both the rich and poor in the Church and within themselves.

This happens best when there is somehow a deep connecting between us, a kind of mutuality in the experience, a union in the mystery of the human condition in the Kingdom of God.

In those moments we take the truth of life as we have encountered it, and, along with the imperfection and poverty and pain, we find beauty and meaning. In this way truth is made into poetry and begins to transform it all.